CALEB ROSS

C 10 Clean architecture with .NET 6

Implementing Clean Architecture with .NET 6

Copyright © 2024 by Caleb Ross

All rights reserved. No part of this publication may be reproduced, stored or transmitted in any form or by any means, electronic, mechanical, photocopying, recording, scanning, or otherwise without written permission from the publisher. It is illegal to copy this book, post it to a website, or distribute it by any other means without permission.

First edition

This book was professionally typeset on Reedsy.
Find out more at reedsy.com

Contents

Introduction	1
Chapter 1: Foundations of Clean Architecture	8
Chapter 2: Setting Up a Clean Architecture Project in .NET 6	15
Chapter 3: Implementing the Domain Layer in Clean...	24
Chapter 4: Implementing the Application Layer in Clean...	35
Chapter 5: Implementing the Infrastructure Layer in Clean...	47
Chapter 6: Implementing the Presentation Layer in Clean...	59
Chapter 7: Testing Strategies for Clean Architecture	69
Chapter 8: Deployment Strategies for Clean Architecture	84
Chapter 9: Scaling and Performance Optimization in Clean...	94
Chapter 10: Security Considerations and Best Practices in...	104
Chapter 11: Event-Driven Architecture and Messaging in Clean...	114
Chapter 12: Integrating External Services and Third-Party...	125
Chapter 13: Deploying and Maintaining Microservices...	135
Chapter 14: Implementing Serverless Architecture in Clean...	145
Chapter 15: Integrating AI and Machine Learning into Clean...	156
Conclusion	166

Introduction

Why Clean Architecture Matters in Modern Software Development

Clean Architecture has revolutionized how software developers approach design and implementation in modern development environments. As businesses increasingly demand scalable, maintainable, and resilient applications, software architects and developers must focus on principles that allow their codebases to adapt to these growing needs.

Clean Architecture is more than just a set of guidelines; it's a framework that helps developers build systems that are:

- **Independent of frameworks**: The system does not rely on the specific tools used to deliver it. Whether you are building an API using ASP.NET Core or a mobile app using Xamarin, the principles remain the same.
- **Testable**: A well-designed clean architecture allows for unit testing, integration testing, and system testing at multiple levels, improving code quality and reducing bugs.
- **Independent of the UI**: Changes in the user interface layer (e.g., from a web interface to a mobile interface) should not require changes to the underlying business logic.
- **Independent of databases or external services**: Whether you use SQL, NoSQL, or a cloud-based solution, Clean Architecture ensures that these choices remain isolated from your core business logic.

- **Maintainable**: As applications grow, technical debt often accumulates, making it difficult to introduce new features without breaking existing ones. Clean Architecture allows developers to make significant changes or add new functionality without disrupting the entire codebase.

One of the key reasons Clean Architecture is gaining traction is due to its ability to address the ever-growing complexity in modern software development. In today's fast-paced digital landscape, applications are expected to perform at scale, be highly responsive, and integrate with various third-party services, often built by globally distributed teams.

With technologies like **C#10** and **.NET 6**, the principles of Clean Architecture are easier to implement. The performance enhancements and language improvements in C#10, combined with the stability of .NET 6, provide an excellent foundation for developers looking to build modern applications without sacrificing maintainability or flexibility.

The Evolution of C# and .NET: Key Changes Leading to C#10 and .NET 6

The evolution of the **C# language** and the **.NET platform** over the years has paved the way for more efficient and cleaner architectures. Understanding the key changes leading to **C#10** and **.NET 6** is essential in fully leveraging the advantages they offer in implementing Clean Architecture.

Early Days of C# and .NET Framework

When C# first appeared in the early 2000s, it was designed to work with the **.NET Framework**, a Windows-only platform. In the early days, developers dealt with more monolithic architecture styles. The focus was on desktop applications, with less emphasis on cross-platform development or cloud integration. However, over the years, as requirements shifted towards more scalable, cloud-friendly applications, both the language and framework needed to evolve.

.NET Core: The Game-Changer

The introduction of **.NET Core** marked a turning point in how the Microsoft ecosystem approached application development. **.NET Core** allowed cross-platform development, opening the doors for Windows,

INTRODUCTION

macOS, and Linux applications. This flexibility enabled developers to consider more diverse architecture patterns and apply them across platforms.

From **C#6** through **C#9**, each iteration brought a wealth of features aimed at simplifying development:

- **C#6** introduced auto-properties and expression-bodied members.
- **C#7** brought pattern matching and local functions.
- **C#8** introduced nullable reference types and async streams, further enhancing code expressiveness and safety.
- **C#9** came with record types, simplifying immutability and improving support for functional programming paradigms.

Each of these changes contributed to building cleaner and more maintainable architectures by reducing boilerplate code, enhancing readability, and offering better support for modern patterns like **Functional Programming** and **Event-Driven Architecture**.

C#10 and .NET 6: The Next Leap Forward

C#10 and **.NET 6** represent the latest evolution in the Microsoft ecosystem, combining performance improvements, language enhancements, and long-term support (LTS) for stability.

Some of the key features in **C#10** include:

- **Global Usings**: No need to write repetitive using directives across multiple files, keeping the code cleaner.
- **File-Scoped Namespaces**: Reducing boilerplate and improving readability by removing the need for braces around namespaces.
- **Record Structs**: Extending the usefulness of records for immutable types but with value semantics.
- **Improvements in Lambda Syntax**: Cleaner and more readable lambda expressions make functional-style coding even easier.

In addition to the language improvements, **.NET 6** brings:

- **Unified Platform**: A single base class library across cloud, desktop, mobile, IoT, and gaming, reducing inconsistencies across platforms.
- **Performance Enhancements**: .NET 6 has been optimized for faster startup times, reduced memory consumption, and more efficient execution. This makes it an ideal platform for building scalable, high-performance applications in Clean Architecture.
- **Long-Term Support (LTS)**: .NET 6 is an LTS release, meaning it will receive security patches and updates for an extended period, making it a reliable choice for enterprise applications.

Who This Book Is For

This book is designed to be a comprehensive guide for software developers and architects who want to implement Clean Architecture using **C#10** and **.NET 6**. Whether you are an experienced developer looking to refine your skills or a newcomer seeking to understand the basics of software architecture, this book will guide you step-by-step through the principles, tools, and techniques necessary to create maintainable and scalable systems.

- **Beginner to Intermediate Developers**: If you're just starting your journey with software architecture, this book will introduce you to key concepts like dependency inversion, separation of concerns, and SOLID principles. You'll learn how to build robust applications using best practices that will stand the test of time.
- **Professional Developers**: For those who already have experience with C# and .NET, this book will offer advanced insights into structuring your projects, optimizing performance, and ensuring maintainability across large-scale applications.
- **Architects and Technical Leads**: As an architect or team lead, you will find useful strategies for scaling applications, managing dependencies, and coordinating between front-end and back-end teams to maintain clean and efficient architecture in large projects.

This book assumes that you have a working knowledge of C# and .NET, but it will provide clear, step-by-step instructions for each architectural concept. Whether you are working on desktop applications, web development, or cloud services, the principles of Clean Architecture will apply.

What You'll Learn: Roadmap to Mastering Clean Architecture with C#10 and .NET 6

This book will walk you through every aspect of building modern, maintainable applications using **Clean Architecture** principles, **C#10** features, and the latest tools in **.NET 6**. Here's a high-level overview of what you'll learn:

1. **Introduction to Clean Architecture**:

- Understand the principles of Clean Architecture, such as separation of concerns and dependency inversion, and how they apply to C# development.

1. **Setting Up Your Project for Success**:

- Learn how to structure your projects in a way that is easy to maintain, extend, and scale.

1. **Mastering the Domain Layer**:

- Explore how to build a domain-driven system with C#10, utilizing techniques such as DDD (Domain-Driven Design) to ensure that your code reflects the business needs.

1. **Implementing Use Cases in the Application Layer**:

- Design clear use cases, decoupling business logic from the infrastructure and UI layers.

1. **Data Access with Entity Framework Core**:

- Learn how to manage data access in a clean architecture by abstracting your database interactions.

1. **Building a Flexible UI Layer**:

- Implement APIs and user interfaces that can change independently of your business logic.

1. **Testing and Validation**:

- Write automated tests that allow you to refactor your code without fear of breaking things.

1. **Advanced C#10 Features**:

- Explore advanced topics like pattern matching, nullable reference types, async streams, and record types, and how they make your architecture cleaner.

1. **Error Handling and Validation**:

- Implement robust error handling and validation strategies to ensure your system behaves as expected even in edge cases.

1. **Performance Optimization and Scaling**:

- Learn about the performance improvements in .NET 6 and how they can help your applications scale effectively.

1. **Security Best Practices**:

- Ensure your architecture is secure from the ground up, covering topics such as authentication, authorization, and data protection.

INTRODUCTION

1. **Deploying Clean Architecture in Production**:

- Understand best practices for deploying your application to the cloud using Docker, Kubernetes, and Azure DevOps.

By the end of this book, you will have the tools and knowledge to confidently build large-scale, high-performance, maintainable applications that stand the test of time.

Setting Up Your Development Environment

Before diving into code and implementation, setting up the right environment is crucial for a smooth development experience. This section will guide you through the necessary tools and configurations.

1. Visual Studio 2022

Visual Studio 2022 is the IDE of choice for most .NET developers, offering a wealth of features, including IntelliSense, debugging, and live unit testing. Make sure you have the latest version installed to leverage the full capabilities of .NET 6 and C#10.

Chapter 1: Foundations of Clean Architecture

Overview of Clean Architecture Principles

Clean Architecture is an architectural pattern created to guide software development toward systems that are easy to maintain, scalable, and flexible. The key idea behind Clean Architecture is to decouple the various parts of a system so that changes in one part don't unnecessarily affect other parts. This isolation of concerns allows a system to be modified or extended over time without breaking existing functionality or requiring massive rewrites.

The primary goal of Clean Architecture is to achieve:

- **Independence of frameworks**: The system's business logic should not depend on any specific frameworks, making it possible to swap frameworks or technologies without changing the core logic.
- **Independence of user interface (UI)**: The business logic should be independent of the UI, allowing developers to change the interface without impacting how the application works internally.
- **Independence of databases or data access layers**: The system should be structured so that database choices and data storage mechanisms are easily replaceable.
- **Testability**: The architecture should make it easy to test the business

logic, allowing for unit tests to be written without relying on external systems like databases or APIs.

At its core, Clean Architecture emphasizes the separation of concerns, where each layer of the system has a specific responsibility. This separation makes it easier to manage complexity, which is a common issue in modern software development. As systems grow, maintaining a clear distinction between business logic, user interface, and infrastructure concerns becomes critical.

Layers of Clean Architecture

In Clean Architecture, the system is typically divided into four primary layers:

1. **Entities (Domain Layer)**: This layer contains the core business logic. It should be the most stable part of the system, containing entities that represent the key business rules.
2. **Use Cases (Application Layer)**: This layer defines the specific actions that can be taken by the system, outlining the flow of data between entities and external components.
3. **Interface Adapters (Presentation Layer)**: This layer is responsible for translating data from the use case layer into a format that the UI can understand and vice versa. It adapts the data from the user input to the application's business rules.
4. **Frameworks and Drivers (Infrastructure Layer)**: This is the outermost layer that handles infrastructure concerns such as databases, APIs, file systems, or any third-party services.

Each of these layers is independent, meaning that changes to one layer do not affect the others. This structure allows for maximum flexibility and scalability.

SOLID Principles: Core to Clean Architecture

The **SOLID principles** are five design principles that are foundational to Clean Architecture. They help maintain clean, maintainable, and scalable codebases by guiding how dependencies should be structured, ensuring high cohesion and low coupling.

1. Single Responsibility Principle (SRP)

The **Single Responsibility Principle** states that a class should have only one reason to change. In other words, each class should have one job or responsibility. This principle prevents classes from becoming too large or taking on too many functions.

In the context of Clean Architecture, SRP applies to how we structure our layers. For example, the business logic should not be responsible for handling database interactions or displaying information in the user interface. Each concern is isolated into its own layer, ensuring that changes in one area don't ripple throughout the system.

2. Open/Closed Principle (OCP)

The **Open/Closed Principle** dictates that classes should be open for extension but closed for modification. This means that you should be able to add new functionality to a class without changing its existing code.

In Clean Architecture, this principle is particularly important when dealing with business rules. Once a rule is established, it should not require modification when new features or functionalities are introduced. Instead, new behavior can be added by extending existing code, ensuring that the core remains unchanged.

3. Liskov Substitution Principle (LSP)

The **Liskov Substitution Principle** ensures that objects of a superclass should be replaceable with objects of a subclass without affecting the correctness of the program.

This principle enforces good inheritance practices, ensuring that derived classes do not override the behavior of their base classes in a way that breaks functionality. In Clean Architecture, this means ensuring that implementations follow contracts laid out by interfaces or abstract classes without deviating from expected behavior.

4. Interface Segregation Principle (ISP)

The **Interface Segregation Principle** states that no client should be forced to depend on methods it does not use. Instead of creating large, monolithic interfaces, it's better to have several smaller interfaces that are specific to the

CHAPTER 1: FOUNDATIONS OF CLEAN ARCHITECTURE

needs of clients.

In Clean Architecture, this principle ensures that each layer has its own well-defined responsibilities and does not require interfaces that span multiple concerns. For example, the infrastructure layer should not have knowledge of the business logic beyond what is necessary for data access.

5. Dependency Inversion Principle (DIP)

The **Dependency Inversion Principle** is arguably the most important principle in Clean Architecture. It states that high-level modules should not depend on low-level modules. Both should depend on abstractions.

In Clean Architecture, this means that business logic (high-level) should not depend on frameworks, databases, or UI (low-level). Instead, it should rely on abstract interfaces that define how communication happens, leaving the implementation details to the outer layers.

By adhering to the SOLID principles, you create a system where concerns are isolated, dependencies are managed through abstractions, and changes to the system are easier to accommodate.

Dependency Inversion and Separation of Concerns
Dependency Inversion

Dependency Inversion is the backbone of Clean Architecture. It requires that high-level policies (business logic) do not depend on low-level details (infrastructure, databases, UI). Instead, both should depend on abstractions.

In Clean Architecture:

- The **core business logic** depends on abstractions such as interfaces that define data access or external services, without knowing how they are implemented.
- The **outer layers** implement those abstractions but do not dictate how the core business logic operates.

For example, if you have a repository interface in the application layer that defines methods for interacting with data, the core business logic would depend on that interface. The actual implementation (whether it's SQL, NoSQL, or a cloud database) would exist in the infrastructure layer.

This separation ensures that changes to the infrastructure do not affect the core business logic, as long as the contract defined by the interface remains the same.

Separation of Concerns

Separation of concerns is the practice of dividing a system into distinct sections, where each section addresses a specific concern. Clean Architecture applies this principle rigorously by breaking the system into independent layers, each with its own responsibility:

- The **domain layer** concerns itself with the core business logic.
- The **application layer** defines use cases that dictate how the system interacts with external components.
- The **interface layer** is responsible for adapting data between the user and the application.
- The **infrastructure layer** deals with the technical details like databases, file systems, and external APIs.

By keeping concerns separated, you make the system more modular and easier to maintain.

How Clean Architecture Solves Common Development Problems

As software systems grow in complexity, they often encounter the following problems:

- **Rigidity**: A system is hard to change because every part of the system is interdependent.
- **Fragility**: Changes in one area can cause unexpected breakages in other areas.
- **Immobility**: Parts of the system cannot be reused in other projects because they are too tightly coupled to specific technologies or implementations.
- **Testability Issues**: Tests become difficult to write because business logic is tightly coupled with external dependencies like databases or APIs.

CHAPTER 1: FOUNDATIONS OF CLEAN ARCHITECTURE

Clean Architecture addresses these problems by:

- **Reducing Coupling**: Through the use of abstractions (interfaces), Clean Architecture ensures that dependencies between layers are minimized. The core business logic doesn't need to know about implementation details.
- **Encouraging Modularity**: Each layer has its own responsibility, making it easier to change or extend specific functionality without affecting the entire system.
- **Improving Testability**: Since the business logic is isolated from external dependencies, unit tests can be written for the core logic without relying on databases or third-party services.
- **Enhancing Maintainability**: With separation of concerns, it becomes easier to maintain the system over time. Bug fixes or feature additions can be made in one area without affecting other parts of the system.

The Structure of Clean Architecture in a .NET 6 Solution

A typical **.NET 6 solution** implementing Clean Architecture will be organized into multiple projects that align with the different layers of the architecture. Here's a breakdown of how the structure could look:

1. **Domain Layer**:

- Contains the core business logic.
- Includes **entities, value objects,** and **domain services**.
- This layer should have no dependencies on external libraries, except for testing purposes.

1. **Application Layer**:

- Contains use cases that coordinate the flow of data between the UI and the domain layer.
- Includes **interfaces** for the infrastructure layer to implement, such as

repositories or external services.
- Depends only on the domain layer and infrastructure abstractions (like repositories).

1. **Infrastructure Layer**:

- Handles database access, file systems, external APIs, and any other external dependencies.
- Implements the interfaces defined in the application layer.

1. **Presentation Layer** (UI/Frontend):

- Responsible for interacting with the user and translating user inputs into use case calls.
- Can be an **ASP.NET Core MVC**, **Blazor** application, or an API.
- The UI layer communicates with the application layer but has no direct access to the domain or infrastructure layers.

By maintaining this structure, you create a solution that adheres to the principles of Clean Architecture, ensuring that each layer is independent, testable, and maintainable over the lifetime of the project.

Chapter 2: Setting Up a Clean Architecture Project in .NET 6

Introduction

In this chapter, we'll focus on how to set up a Clean Architecture project using .NET 6 and C#10. The goal is to create a solid foundation that you can build upon as you implement the principles discussed in the previous chapter. Clean Architecture encourages a modular, layered approach to structuring projects, ensuring scalability, testability, and maintainability. By the end of this chapter, you will have a well-organized solution structure ready for Clean Architecture implementation.

Section 1: Overview of Project Setup

Before we dive into the technical steps, let's discuss the general structure and goals of a Clean Architecture solution. At a high level, the project will be divided into four key layers:

1. **Domain Layer**: The core of the application, containing business logic and domain entities. This layer should have no dependencies on other layers or external frameworks.
2. **Application Layer**: This layer contains use cases, business rules, and interfaces for interacting with infrastructure and presentation layers.

3. **Infrastructure Layer**: Responsible for implementing external services, database access, logging, and other framework-related services.
4. **Presentation Layer**: The user interface, which could be a web app, mobile app, or an API, interacts with the application layer.

Each of these layers will exist in separate projects, ensuring clear boundaries and dependencies.

Section 2: Setting Up the Development Environment

To start building a Clean Architecture project, you'll need to set up a modern .NET 6 development environment. This section will cover installing the necessary tools and ensuring that the environment is optimized for development.

Tools You'll Need

- **Visual Studio 2022**: As the flagship IDE for .NET development, Visual Studio 2022 provides extensive support for .NET 6 and C#10. Ensure you have the latest version installed to access all the new features and improvements.
- **.NET SDK 6**: .NET 6 SDK is essential for building applications with the latest framework.
- **NuGet Packages**: Several NuGet packages will be required for Clean Architecture, such as Entity Framework Core, MediatR, FluentValidation, and more.

Step-by-step installation guides can include:

- **Visual Studio Setup**: Guide users through setting up the environment with all necessary components (ASP.NET Core, Blazor, etc.).
- **.NET SDK**: Instructions on installing the .NET 6 SDK for different operating systems.

CHAPTER 2: SETTING UP A CLEAN ARCHITECTURE PROJECT IN .NET 6

Section 3: Creating the Solution Structure

Now that the environment is ready, it's time to set up the solution structure. In Clean Architecture, the solution is organized into multiple projects that align with the core layers of the architecture.

Step-by-Step Guide to Project Creation

1. **Creating a Solution in Visual Studio**

- Start by creating a new solution in Visual Studio. Select **Empty Solution** to avoid boilerplate code and retain control over how the solution is organized.
- Name your solution appropriately, for example, CleanArchitectureApp.

1. **Adding Core Projects**

- **Domain Project**: This project will contain the core entities and business logic. Right-click the solution, add a new project, and select **Class Library**. Name it CleanArchitecture.Domain.
- **Application Project**: The application project will define the use cases and business rules. Add a new **Class Library** project called CleanArchitecture.Application.
- **Infrastructure Project**: This project will handle database access and any other external dependencies. Add a **Class Library** project named CleanArchitecture.Infrastructure.
- **Presentation Project**: This will be your front-end project (either a web application or an API). For example, if you are building an API, add an **ASP.NET Core Web API** project called CleanArchitecture.WebAPI.

1. **Setting Up References**

- Add the necessary project references so that the layers can interact correctly:

- CleanArchitecture.Application references CleanArchitecture.Domain.
- CleanArchitecture.Infrastructure references CleanArchitecture.Application and CleanArchitecture.Domain.
- CleanArchitecture.WebAPI references CleanArchitecture.Application.

At this point, you will have a modular solution structure that adheres to Clean Architecture principles.

Section 4: Implementing the Domain Layer

Core Concepts of the Domain Layer

The **Domain Layer** is the heart of the system, and it should not have any dependencies on external frameworks or databases. The entities and value objects within this layer represent the core business logic.

Entities

Entities represent key business objects that contain domain logic and behaviors. An entity typically has an identity, which makes it distinct from other objects.

Example: Defining an Entity

```csharp
Copy code
public class Product
{
    public int Id { get; set; }
    public string Name { get; private set; }
    public decimal Price { get; private set; }

    public Product(string name, decimal price)
    {
        Name = name;
        Price = price;
    }

    public void UpdatePrice(decimal newPrice)
```

CHAPTER 2: SETTING UP A CLEAN ARCHITECTURE PROJECT IN .NET 6

```
    {
        Price = newPrice;
    }
}
```

Value Objects

Value objects differ from entities in that they don't have an identity. Instead, they are defined by their properties.

Example: Creating a Value Object

```csharp
Copy code
public class Money
{
    public decimal Amount { get; }
    public string Currency { get; }

    public Money(decimal amount, string currency)
    {
        Amount = amount;
        Currency = currency;
    }
}
```

Domain Events

Domain events capture important business events that occur within the domain. These events are often used to notify other parts of the system when significant changes occur.

Section 5: Building the Application Layer

The **Application Layer** manages use cases and handles the orchestration of domain logic. It defines how the system interacts with external systems, repositories, and the domain entities.

Use Cases and Services

Each use case represents a specific action that the application can perform.

C 10 CLEAN ARCHITECTURE WITH .NET 6

These use cases encapsulate business logic and delegate to domain entities.

Example: Creating a Use Case

```csharp
Copy code
public class CreateOrderCommand
{
    public int ProductId { get; set; }
    public int Quantity { get; set; }
}

public class CreateOrderHandler : IRequestHandler<CreateOrderCommand, bool>
{
    private readonly IProductRepository _productRepository;

    public CreateOrderHandler(IProductRepository productRepository)
    {
        _productRepository = productRepository;
    }

    public async Task<bool> Handle(CreateOrderCommand request, CancellationToken cancellationToken)
    {
        var product = await _productRepository.GetProductById(request.ProductId);

        if (product == null)
        {
            return false;
        }

        var order = new Order(product, request.Quantity);
        await _productRepository.AddOrder(order);

        return true;
    }
}
```

MediatR for Decoupling Use Cases

CHAPTER 2: SETTING UP A CLEAN ARCHITECTURE PROJECT IN .NET 6

MediatR is a popular library used to decouple requests from the handling of business logic. It allows use cases to be managed independently and improves separation of concerns.

Section 6: Implementing the Infrastructure Layer

The **Infrastructure Layer** provides implementations for services such as database access, file storage, and external APIs. It depends on the application layer interfaces but does not affect the core business logic.

Database Access with Entity Framework Core

Entity Framework Core is commonly used for database access in .NET applications. The infrastructure layer will include implementations of repositories and data services.

Example: Implementing a Repository

```csharp
Copy code
public class ProductRepository : IProductRepository
{
    private readonly AppDbContext _context;

    public ProductRepository(AppDbContext context)
    {
        _context = context;
    }

    public async Task<Product> GetProductById(int productId)
    {
        return await _context.Products.FindAsync(productId);
    }

    public async Task AddOrder(Order order)
    {
        await _context.Orders.AddAsync(order);
        await _context.SaveChangesAsync();
    }
```

}

Dependency Injection in .NET 6

The **Infrastructure Layer** is where services such as repositories are registered with the dependency injection container. This allows them to be injected into the application layer as needed.

Section 7: Setting Up the Presentation Layer

The **Presentation Layer** serves as the user interface or API that interacts with the outside world. For a web API, you will use ASP.NET Core to build this layer.

Configuring ASP.NET Core

Set up the API to handle HTTP requests and route them to the appropriate use cases.

Example: Creating an API Controller

```csharp
Copy code
[ApiController]
[Route("api/[controller]")]
public class ProductsController : ControllerBase
{
    private readonly IMediator _mediator;

    public ProductsController(IMediator mediator)
    {
        _mediator = mediator;
    }

    [HttpPost]
    public async Task<IActionResult> CreateOrder([FromBody] CreateOrderCommand command)
    {
        var result = await _mediator.Send(command);
```

```
        if (result)
        {
            return Ok();
        }

        return BadRequest();
    }
}
```

Middleware and Validation

ASP.NET Core provides middleware for cross-cutting concerns such as authentication, authorization, and validation. FluentValidation can be integrated to ensure data is valid before reaching the application layer.

Conclusion

At this point, you should have a fully structured Clean Architecture project, with well-defined layers and responsibilities. The key takeaway from this chapter is that proper project structure is essential for maintaining clean, scalable, and testable code. By organizing your code into distinct layers, you ensure that each part of your system is decoupled and can evolve independently.

This chapter sets the foundation for further implementation of Clean Architecture in the following chapters, where we'll dive deeper into each layer and explore advanced concepts such as CQRS, testing, and performance optimization.

Chapter 3: Implementing the Domain Layer in Clean Architecture

Introduction

The **Domain Layer** is the foundation of Clean Architecture. It encapsulates the core business logic and represents the most stable part of the system. Unlike other layers, which may interact with external systems or frameworks, the domain layer is purely focused on representing business rules, entities, and core behaviors. This chapter will explore how to build a robust domain layer, following Clean Architecture principles, using **C#10** and **.NET 6**.

By the end of this chapter, you will have a thorough understanding of:
- The role of the domain layer in Clean Architecture.
- How to define entities, value objects, aggregates, and domain events.
- Best practices for structuring your domain model.
- How the domain layer is independent of the infrastructure and other concerns.

CHAPTER 3: IMPLEMENTING THE DOMAIN LAYER IN CLEAN...

Section 1: Understanding the Role of the Domain Layer

The **Domain Layer** is the centerpiece of Clean Architecture. Its primary responsibility is to capture and enforce business rules and logic. This layer should be highly cohesive and isolated from external systems, which means it should not depend on infrastructure, UI, or database systems. Changes to these external systems should not affect the core business logic.

In essence, the **Domain Layer** contains the "why" of the system. It represents the **business rules** and **policies** that dictate how the system behaves. Any code within this layer should be directly tied to the rules and requirements of the business.

Key Principles of the Domain Layer:

1. **Business Logic Only**: This layer contains business entities, rules, and behaviors—nothing else.
2. **Independence from Frameworks**: It does not rely on any infrastructure, libraries, or frameworks (other than maybe a few core libraries like System).
3. **High Cohesion**: The domain layer should consist of tightly related components, meaning that each piece serves a specific and vital role within the business model.
4. **Entities and Value Objects**: These are central to the domain model and represent the fundamental concepts of the business.

Core Components of the Domain Layer

- **Entities**: Objects that have a distinct identity and encapsulate business rules. They are the core actors in your system.
- **Value Objects**: Immutable objects that are defined by their properties and don't have an identity of their own.
- **Aggregates**: Groups of related entities and value objects that are treated as a single unit.
- **Domain Services**: Operations that are too complex to fit within a single

entity but are part of the core business logic.
- **Domain Events**: Events that indicate something significant has happened within the domain.

Section 2: Defining Entities in the Domain Layer

Entities are central to the domain model in Clean Architecture. Each entity represents a core concept in the business, such as a product, order, or customer. What makes an entity distinct is its **identity**. Entities have unique identifiers and can change over time while retaining the same identity.

Best Practices for Designing Entities

1. **Encapsulation**: All business rules and behaviors should be encapsulated within entities. For example, if an entity represents an Order, it should handle operations such as adding items to the order or applying discounts.
2. **Consistency**: Entities should maintain consistent and valid states throughout their lifecycle.
3. **Identity**: Each entity should have a unique identifier (e.g., an Id) that distinguishes it from other entities.

Let's dive into an example. Imagine we're building an e-commerce system. One of the most important entities is the **Product**.

Example: Defining an Entity in C#10

```csharp
Copy code
public class Product
{
    public int Id { get; private set; }
    public string Name { get; private set; }
    public decimal Price { get; private set; }
    public int StockQuantity { get; private set; }
```

```csharp
    public Product(string name, decimal price, int stockQuantity)
    {
        if (string.IsNullOrEmpty(name))
            throw new ArgumentException("Product name cannot be
            empty.");

        if (price <= 0)
            throw new ArgumentException("Price must be greater
            than zero.");

        Name = name;
        Price = price;
        StockQuantity = stockQuantity;
    }

    public void UpdatePrice(decimal newPrice)
    {
        if (newPrice <= 0)
            throw new ArgumentException("Price must be greater
            than zero.");

        Price = newPrice;
    }

    public void ReduceStock(int quantity)
    {
        if (quantity > StockQuantity)
            throw new InvalidOperationException("Not enough stock
            available.");

        StockQuantity -= quantity;
    }
}
```

In this example, the Product entity is responsible for managing its own state. It contains business rules that ensure that a product can never have a negative price or reduce stock beyond what is available.

Section 3: Understanding Value Objects

Value Objects are another key part of the domain model. Unlike entities, value objects do not have an identity. They are defined entirely by their attributes, which makes them perfect for concepts such as currency, addresses, or dates.

Characteristics of Value Objects:

1. **Immutability**: Once created, value objects cannot change. If you need to update a value object, you create a new instance.
2. **Equality Based on Attributes**: Two value objects are equal if all their properties are the same.
3. **No Identity**: Value objects do not have an identity the way entities do.

Example: Creating a Value Object

In an e-commerce application, a value object could represent **Money**. Money consists of an amount and a currency, and it's immutable.

```csharp
Copy code
public class Money
{
    public decimal Amount { get; }
    public string Currency { get; }

    public Money(decimal amount, string currency)
    {
        if (amount < 0)
            throw new ArgumentException("Amount cannot be
            negative.");

        if (string.IsNullOrEmpty(currency))
            throw new ArgumentException("Currency cannot be
            empty.");

        Amount = amount;
```

CHAPTER 3: IMPLEMENTING THE DOMAIN LAYER IN CLEAN...

```
        Currency = currency;
    }

    public Money Add(Money other)
    {
        if (other.Currency != Currency)
            throw new InvalidOperationException("Cannot add
            amounts with different currencies.");

        return new Money(Amount + other.Amount, Currency);
    }
}
```

In this example, the Money value object ensures that you can't mix currencies and that once a Money object is created, its value can't be changed. You can only create new Money objects based on existing ones.

Why Use Value Objects?

Value objects simplify your domain model by grouping related properties together and ensuring that they behave correctly. For example, when you use a Money value object, you can be confident that you won't end up with invalid currency amounts or inconsistent values.

Section 4: Aggregates in Clean Architecture

An **Aggregate** is a group of related entities and value objects that are treated as a single unit within the domain. The most important thing to understand about aggregates is that they ensure **consistency** within the group of entities. Each aggregate has a **root entity** that controls access to other entities in the group.

Why Use Aggregates?

Aggregates ensure that related entities are kept in sync and follow the same business rules. For example, in an e-commerce system, an **Order** may be an aggregate that includes multiple **Order Items**. The **Order** entity is responsible for managing the items and ensuring that business rules are enforced across the entire order.

Example: Defining an Aggregate Root

```csharp
Copy code
public class Order
{
    public int Id { get; private set; }
    public List<OrderItem> Items { get; private set; }
    public decimal TotalAmount => Items.Sum(item =>
    item.TotalPrice);

    public Order()
    {
        Items = new List<OrderItem>();
    }

    public void AddItem(Product product, int quantity)
    {
        if (quantity <= 0)
            throw new ArgumentException("Quantity must be greater
            than zero.");

        var orderItem = new OrderItem(product, quantity);
        Items.Add(orderItem);
    }
}

public class OrderItem
{
    public int Id { get; private set; }
    public Product Product { get; private set; }
    public int Quantity { get; private set; }
    public decimal TotalPrice => Product.Price * Quantity;

    public OrderItem(Product product, int quantity)
    {
        Product = product;
        Quantity = quantity;
    }
}
```

CHAPTER 3: IMPLEMENTING THE DOMAIN LAYER IN CLEAN...

In this example, the Order entity acts as the **aggregate root**, managing the OrderItem entities. The Order entity is responsible for ensuring that the items in the order are valid and follow the business rules. This setup ensures that changes to the items (such as adding or removing items) are managed by the root entity.

Consistency in Aggregates

One of the key responsibilities of an aggregate is to maintain **consistency** across its entities. For example, an order aggregate might enforce rules such as "an order cannot be placed with a total amount of zero." By encapsulating these rules within the aggregate, you ensure that the entire group of entities behaves as a single, consistent unit.

Section 5: Domain Services

In some cases, certain business logic doesn't fit neatly into a single entity or aggregate. For example, some operations might involve multiple aggregates or complex calculations that span several entities. In these cases, **Domain Services** come into play.

Characteristics of Domain Services:

- **Stateless**: Domain services do not maintain any internal state.
- **Business Logic**: They encapsulate business logic that spans multiple entities or aggregates.

Example: Defining a Domain Service

```csharp
csharp
Copy code
public class ShippingService
{
    public decimal CalculateShippingCost(Order order)
    {
        const decimal baseCost = 10m;
```

```csharp
        if (order.TotalAmount > 100m)
        {
            return 0m; // Free shipping for orders over $100.
        }

        return baseCost;
    }
}
```

In this example, the ShippingService handles the calculation of shipping costs for an order. This logic doesn't belong to any specific entity and instead applies to the order as a whole, which makes it a good candidate for a domain service.

Section 6: Domain Events in Clean Architecture

Domain Events represent significant events that occur within the domain. For example, if an order is placed or a product's price is updated, these are events that other parts of the system might be interested in.

Why Use Domain Events?

Domain events allow the system to notify other parts of the application when something important happens. They decouple the domain logic from other layers by allowing the domain to publish events that can be handled by other systems (such as sending emails or updating external systems).

Example: Creating a Domain Event

```
csharp
Copy code
public class OrderPlacedEvent : IDomainEvent
{
    public Order Order { get; private set; }

    public OrderPlacedEvent(Order order)
    {
        Order = order;
```

        }
}

Publishing Domain Events

In Clean Architecture, domain events are typically published by the aggregate root. When a significant event occurs (such as an order being placed), the aggregate publishes an event that can be handled by other parts of the system.

Section 7: Structuring the Domain Layer in .NET 6

Now that we've covered the key components of the domain layer, let's discuss how to structure your **.NET 6** project to keep your domain logic clean and organized.

Suggested Structure for the Domain Layer:

- **Entities**: A folder that contains all of your domain entities.
- **ValueObjects**: A folder for your value objects.
- **Aggregates**: A folder for aggregate root classes.
- **DomainEvents**: A folder to store all domain events.
- **Services**: A folder for domain services that encapsulate logic beyond a single entity.

Your domain layer should be free from dependencies on external libraries. It should only contain business logic, entities, and value objects.

Conclusion

The domain layer is the core of Clean Architecture and is essential for ensuring that business rules and logic are encapsulated in a clean, maintainable way. By following the principles of Clean Architecture, you can build a domain layer that is independent, testable, and highly cohesive.

In this chapter, we've explored how to define entities, value objects, aggregates, domain services, and domain events. In the next chapter, we'll focus on implementing the application layer, which orchestrates the flow of data and use cases, bridging the domain and infrastructure layers.

Chapter 4: Implementing the Application Layer in Clean Architecture

Introduction

The **Application Layer** is where the orchestration of business logic occurs in a Clean Architecture solution. It is responsible for defining the use cases of the application and managing the interactions between the domain layer and external systems. While the domain layer encapsulates the business rules, the application layer dictates how these rules are applied in specific scenarios, ensuring that data flows smoothly through the system.

In this chapter, you will learn how to:
- Structure the application layer effectively.
- Implement use cases that encapsulate business logic.
- Use MediatR to handle commands and queries.
- Manage transactions and workflows across aggregates.
- Validate user input and ensure that the application layer remains clean and maintainable.

Section 1: Overview of the Application Layer

The Application Layer serves as the bridge between the user interface and the domain layer. Its main responsibilities include:

1. **Use Case Management**: Defining and executing use cases that represent the actions users can take within the application.
2. **Coordination**: Orchestrating the interactions between the domain layer, infrastructure, and presentation layers.
3. **Input Validation**: Ensuring that data passed into the system meets business rules before invoking domain logic.
4. **Transaction Management**: Handling the lifecycle of transactions across aggregates, ensuring data consistency and integrity.

The application layer should be free of business logic itself; instead, it coordinates and delegates the necessary actions to the domain layer.

Section 2: Structuring the Application Layer

When implementing the application layer, it's essential to maintain a clear structure that aligns with Clean Architecture principles. Here's a suggested structure for the **Application Layer** in a .NET 6 solution:

Suggested Folder Structure

- **Commands**: Contains command definitions and handlers for creating or modifying data.
- **Queries**: Contains query definitions and handlers for retrieving data.
- **DTOs**: Data Transfer Objects used for passing data between layers, especially for input/output.
- **Interfaces**: Interface definitions for repositories and services that will be implemented in the infrastructure layer.
- **Services**: Application-level services that coordinate operations involving multiple domain entities.

This structure promotes clarity and separation of concerns, making it easier to manage the growing complexity of your application as it evolves.

Section 3: Implementing Use Cases

In the application layer, each use case corresponds to a specific action or operation that a user can perform. Use cases encapsulate all the necessary interactions to complete a task and validate input data.

Defining a Use Case

A use case typically includes:

- Input validation.
- Calling the appropriate domain logic.
- Handling exceptions and returning results.

Example: Create Order Use Case

Let's walk through the implementation of a use case for creating an order.

1. **Define the Command**: The command represents the input for the use case.

```csharp
Copy code
public class CreateOrderCommand
{
    public int ProductId { get; set; }
    public int Quantity { get; set; }
}
```

1. **Create the Command Handler**: This handler processes the command and interacts with the domain layer.

```csharp
Copy code
public class CreateOrderHandler :
IRequestHandler<CreateOrderCommand, int>
{
    private readonly IOrderRepository _orderRepository;
    private readonly IProductRepository _productRepository;

    public CreateOrderHandler(IOrderRepository orderRepository,
    IProductRepository productRepository)
    {
        _orderRepository = orderRepository;
        _productRepository = productRepository;
    }

    public async Task<int> Handle(CreateOrderCommand request,
    CancellationToken cancellationToken)
    {
        var product = await
        _productRepository.GetProductById(request.ProductId);
        if (product == null)
            throw new NotFoundException($"Product with ID
            {request.ProductId} not found.");

        var order = new Order();
        order.AddItem(product, request.Quantity);
        await _orderRepository.AddAsync(order);

        return order.Id; // Return the created order ID.
    }
}
```

1. **Register the Command Handler**: In your dependency injection setup, ensure that the command handler is registered.

CHAPTER 4: IMPLEMENTING THE APPLICATION LAYER IN CLEAN...

```csharp
Copy code
services.AddMediatR(typeof(CreateOrderHandler).Assembly);
```

Section 4: Using MediatR for Command and Query Handling

MediatR is a popular library that simplifies the implementation of the mediator pattern in .NET applications. It allows for loose coupling between components, making the application layer cleaner and more maintainable.

Setting Up MediatR

To get started with MediatR, install the package via NuGet:

```csharp
Copy code
dotnet add package MediatR
```

Once installed, you can use MediatR to handle commands and queries seamlessly.

Handling Queries

Similar to commands, queries can be defined and handled in the application layer.

Example: Defining a Query

```csharp
Copy code
public class GetOrderByIdQuery : IRequest<OrderDto>
{
    public int OrderId { get; set; }

    public GetOrderByIdQuery(int orderId)
    {
        OrderId = orderId;
    }
```

39

}

Query Handler Implementation

```csharp
Copy code
public class GetOrderByIdHandler : 
IRequestHandler<GetOrderByIdQuery, OrderDto>
{
    private readonly IOrderRepository _orderRepository;

    public GetOrderByIdHandler(IOrderRepository orderRepository)
    {
        _orderRepository = orderRepository;
    }

    public async Task<OrderDto> Handle(GetOrderByIdQuery request, 
    CancellationToken cancellationToken)
    {
        var order = await 
        _orderRepository.GetByIdAsync(request.OrderId);
        if (order == null)
            throw new NotFoundException($"Order with ID 
            {request.OrderId} not found.");

        return new OrderDto
        {
            Id = order.Id,
            Items = order.Items.Select(item => new OrderItemDto
            {
                ProductId = item.Product.Id,
                Quantity = item.Quantity
            }).ToList(),
            TotalAmount = order.TotalAmount
        };
    }
}
```

CHAPTER 4: IMPLEMENTING THE APPLICATION LAYER IN CLEAN...

Section 5: Input Validation in the Application Layer

Input validation is critical in ensuring that only valid data is passed into the domain layer. The application layer is responsible for validating incoming commands and queries before they are processed.

Implementing Validation

Using libraries like **FluentValidation** can simplify the validation process.

1. **Install FluentValidation**

```bash
Copy code
dotnet add package FluentValidation
```

1. **Create a Validator for Your Command**

```csharp
Copy code
public class CreateOrderCommandValidator : AbstractValidator<CreateOrderCommand>
{
    public CreateOrderCommandValidator()
    {
        RuleFor(x => x.ProductId).GreaterThan(0).WithMessage("Product ID must be greater than zero.");
        RuleFor(x => x.Quantity).GreaterThan(0).WithMessage("Quantity must be greater than zero.");
    }
}
```

1. **Integrate Validation in the Command Handler** Before handling the command, validate it to ensure it meets business rules.

```csharp
Copy code
public class CreateOrderHandler :
IRequestHandler<CreateOrderCommand, int>
{
    private readonly IOrderRepository _orderRepository;
    private readonly IProductRepository _productRepository;
    private readonly IValidator<CreateOrderCommand> _validator;

    public CreateOrderHandler(IOrderRepository orderRepository,
    IProductRepository productRepository,
    IValidator<CreateOrderCommand> validator)
    {
        _orderRepository = orderRepository;
        _productRepository = productRepository;
        _validator = validator;
    }

    public async Task<int> Handle(CreateOrderCommand request,
    CancellationToken cancellationToken)
    {
        var validationResult = await
        _validator.ValidateAsync(request);
        if (!validationResult.IsValid)
            throw new ValidationException(validationResult.Errors);

        // Proceed with command handling...
    }
}
```

Section 6: Transaction Management

Managing transactions is crucial for maintaining data consistency, especially when multiple operations must succeed or fail together. The application layer can leverage the **Unit of Work** pattern to manage transactions.

Implementing the Unit of Work Pattern

1. **Define a Unit of Work Interface**

```csharp
Copy code
public interface IUnitOfWork
{
    Task<int> SaveChangesAsync();
}
```

1. **Implement the Unit of Work**

```csharp
Copy code
public class UnitOfWork : IUnitOfWork
{
    private readonly AppDbContext _context;

    public UnitOfWork(AppDbContext context)
    {
        _context = context;
    }

    public async Task<int> SaveChangesAsync()
    {
        return await _context.SaveChangesAsync();
    }
```

}

1. **Using Unit of Work in the Command Handler** Ensure that changes are committed only if the command executes successfully.

```csharp
Copy code
public class CreateOrderHandler :
IRequestHandler<CreateOrderCommand, int>
{
    private readonly IOrderRepository _orderRepository;
    private readonly IProductRepository _productRepository;
    private readonly IUnitOfWork _unitOfWork;

    public CreateOrderHandler(IOrderRepository orderRepository,
    IProductRepository productRepository, IUnitOfWork unitOfWork)
    {
        _orderRepository = orderRepository;
        _productRepository = productRepository;
        _unitOfWork = unitOfWork;
    }

    public async Task<int> Handle(CreateOrderCommand request,
    CancellationToken cancellationToken)
    {
        var product = await
        _productRepository.GetProductById(request.ProductId);
        if (product == null)
            throw new NotFoundException($"Product with ID
            {request.ProductId} not found.");

        var order = new Order();
        order.AddItem(product, request.Quantity);
        await _orderRepository.AddAsync(order);

        await _unitOfWork.SaveChangesAsync();
```

```
        return order.Id;
    }
}
```

Section 7: Integrating the Application Layer with Other Layers

The application layer interacts closely with both the domain layer and the infrastructure layer. It defines the boundaries between these layers and facilitates communication between them.

Communication with the Domain Layer

The application layer communicates with the domain layer by invoking methods on entities, aggregates, and domain services. It orchestrates the execution of business logic and ensures that all necessary operations are performed in a coherent manner.

Interfacing with the Infrastructure Layer

The application layer depends on interfaces defined in the application layer for repositories and services that are implemented in the infrastructure layer. This allows for a clean separation of concerns, making it easy to switch implementations without affecting the core business logic.

Conclusion

In this chapter, we have explored the crucial role of the application layer in Clean Architecture. We covered how to structure the application layer, implement use cases, manage commands and queries with MediatR, validate user input, and handle transactions.

The application layer serves as the orchestration hub, coordinating interactions between the user interface, domain logic, and infrastructure. By adhering to Clean Architecture principles, you ensure that your application is maintainable, testable, and scalable.

In the next chapter, we will delve into the infrastructure layer, exploring how to implement database access, external services, and how this layer interacts with both the application and domain layers.

Chapter 5: Implementing the Infrastructure Layer in Clean Architecture

Introduction

The **Infrastructure Layer** is a critical component of Clean Architecture, responsible for all external interactions and technical concerns that do not belong in the domain or application layers. This includes data persistence, external service integrations, logging, and any other frameworks or technologies required by the application. The main goal of the infrastructure layer is to provide concrete implementations for the abstractions defined in the application layer while ensuring that these implementations do not pollute the domain model.

In this chapter, you will learn:
- The role and responsibilities of the infrastructure layer.
- How to implement database access using Entity Framework Core.
- How to work with external services.
- Best practices for managing infrastructure concerns.
- How to ensure that the infrastructure layer remains decoupled from the domain layer.

Section 1: Overview of the Infrastructure Layer

The infrastructure layer serves as the bridge between the application and the external world. It is responsible for implementing the technical details required by the application, such as:

- **Data Access**: Interacting with databases and managing data persistence.
- **External Service Integration**: Connecting to APIs or third-party services.
- **Logging and Monitoring**: Capturing application behavior and performance.
- **File Storage**: Handling file uploads and downloads.

Characteristics of the Infrastructure Layer

1. **Implementation of Interfaces**: The infrastructure layer should implement the interfaces defined in the application layer, ensuring that the application remains decoupled from the details of the infrastructure.
2. **No Business Logic**: Business logic should never reside in the infrastructure layer; it should only contain the technical details needed to support the application.
3. **Flexibility**: The infrastructure layer should allow for easy swapping of implementations without affecting the application or domain layers.

Section 2: Setting Up Entity Framework Core for Data Access

Entity Framework Core (EF Core) is a powerful Object-Relational Mapper (ORM) that simplifies data access in .NET applications. This section will guide you through setting up EF Core in your Clean Architecture project.

Step 1: Install Entity Framework Core Packages

To use EF Core, you need to install the necessary NuGet packages. You can do this using the Package Manager Console or by editing your .csproj file.

Using the Package Manager Console:

CHAPTER 5: IMPLEMENTING THE INFRASTRUCTURE LAYER IN CLEAN...

```bash
Copy code
dotnet add package Microsoft.EntityFrameworkCore
dotnet add package Microsoft.EntityFrameworkCore.SqlServer
dotnet add package Microsoft.EntityFrameworkCore.Tools
```

Step 2: Creating the Database Context

The database context is the primary class that coordinates EF Core functionality for a given data model. It manages entity objects during runtime and handles database operations.

Example: Creating a DbContext

```csharp
Copy code
public class AppDbContext : DbContext
{
    public AppDbContext(DbContextOptions<AppDbContext> options) : base(options)
    {
    }

    public DbSet<Product> Products { get; set; }
    public DbSet<Order> Orders { get; set; }

    protected override void OnModelCreating(ModelBuilder modelBuilder)
    {
        // Configure entity mappings and relationships here.
    }
}
```

Step 3: Configuring Dependency Injection

You need to configure the dependency injection container in your Startup.cs or Program.cs file to use the AppDbContext.

```csharp
Copy code
services.AddDbContext<AppDbContext>(options =>
    options.UseSqlServer(Configuration.GetConnectionString("DefaultConnection")));
```

Step 4: Managing Migrations

Entity Framework Core provides a migration feature that allows you to update the database schema to match your data model. You can create and apply migrations using the command line.

Creating a Migration

```bash
Copy code
dotnet ef migrations add InitialCreate
```

Updating the Database

```bash
Copy code
dotnet ef database update
```

This process helps you keep your database schema in sync with your entity models.

Section 3: Implementing Repositories for Data Access

Repositories act as an abstraction layer between the domain and the data access layer. They encapsulate data access logic, allowing the application layer to work with a clean interface.

Defining Repository Interfaces

Define repository interfaces in the application layer to abstract data operations. For example, the IProductRepository interface might look like

CHAPTER 5: IMPLEMENTING THE INFRASTRUCTURE LAYER IN CLEAN...

this:

```csharp
Copy code
public interface IProductRepository
{
    Task<Product> GetProductById(int productId);
    Task<IEnumerable<Product>> GetAllProducts();
    Task AddAsync(Product product);
}
```

Implementing Repositories in the Infrastructure Layer

In the infrastructure layer, implement the repository interfaces defined in the application layer.

Example: Implementing Product Repository

```csharp
Copy code
public class ProductRepository : IProductRepository
{
    private readonly AppDbContext _context;

    public ProductRepository(AppDbContext context)
    {
        _context = context;
    }

    public async Task<Product> GetProductById(int productId)
    {
        return await _context.Products.FindAsync(productId);
    }

    public async Task<IEnumerable<Product>> GetAllProducts()
    {
        return await _context.Products.ToListAsync();
    }

    public async Task AddAsync(Product product)
    {
```

```
        await _context.Products.AddAsync(product);
        await _context.SaveChangesAsync();
    }
}
```

This implementation provides data access methods that the application layer can call without being aware of how data is stored or retrieved.

Section 4: Integrating External Services

In many applications, integrating with external services is essential. Whether it's a payment gateway, an email service, or a third-party API, the infrastructure layer is where these integrations occur.

Defining External Service Interfaces

Similar to repositories, define interfaces for external services in the application layer.

Example: Payment Service Interface

```csharp
Copy code
public interface IPaymentService
{
    Task<bool> ProcessPayment(decimal amount, string
    paymentMethod);
}
```

Implementing External Services

Implement the interface in the infrastructure layer, handling the specifics of the integration.

Example: Implementing Payment Service

```csharp
Copy code
```

CHAPTER 5: IMPLEMENTING THE INFRASTRUCTURE LAYER IN CLEAN...

```csharp
public class PaymentService : IPaymentService
{
    public async Task<bool> ProcessPayment(decimal amount, string paymentMethod)
    {
        // Logic to integrate with payment gateway API
        // For example, call an external payment processing API
        return true; // Return true if payment is successful
    }
}
```

Using External Services in the Application Layer

Once implemented, external services can be injected into the application layer, allowing use cases to utilize them seamlessly.

Example: Using Payment Service in a Use Case

```csharp
Copy code
public class CheckoutHandler : IRequestHandler<CheckoutCommand>
{
    private readonly IPaymentService _paymentService;

    public CheckoutHandler(IPaymentService paymentService)
    {
        _paymentService = paymentService;
    }

    public async Task Handle(CheckoutCommand request, CancellationToken cancellationToken)
    {
        // Perform checkout logic
        var success = await _paymentService.ProcessPayment(request.Amount, request.PaymentMethod);

        if (!success)
        {
```

53

```
            throw new Exception("Payment failed.");
        }
    }
}
```

Section 5: Logging and Monitoring in the Infrastructure Layer

Logging is an essential aspect of any application, allowing you to monitor behavior, diagnose issues, and track performance. The infrastructure layer is where logging is typically configured and implemented.

Setting Up Logging in .NET 6

.NET Core provides built-in support for logging through the Microsoft.Extensions.Logging namespace. To set up logging:

1. **Configure Logging in Program.cs or Startup.cs**:

```csharp
Copy code
public static IHostBuilder CreateHostBuilder(string[] args) =>
    Host.CreateDefaultBuilder(args)
        .ConfigureLogging(logging =>
        {
            logging.ClearProviders();
            logging.AddConsole();
            logging.AddDebug();
        })
        .ConfigureWebHostDefaults(webBuilder =>
        {
            webBuilder.UseStartup<Startup>();
        });
```

1. **Injecting the Logger into Classes**: You can inject ILogger<T> into your classes for logging purposes.

Example: Using Logging in a Repository

```csharp
Copy code
public class ProductRepository : IProductRepository
{
    private readonly AppDbContext _context;
    private readonly ILogger<ProductRepository> _logger;

    public ProductRepository(AppDbContext context,
    ILogger<ProductRepository> logger)
    {
        _context = context;
        _logger = logger;
    }

    public async Task<Product> GetProductById(int productId)
    {
        _logger.LogInformation("Fetching product with ID
        {ProductId}", productId);
        return await _context.Products.FindAsync(productId);
    }
}
```

Section 6: Testing the Infrastructure Layer

Testing is crucial for maintaining the integrity and reliability of the infrastructure layer. By writing tests for the infrastructure components, you ensure that your data access and external integrations function correctly.

Unit Testing Repositories

Use a testing framework like **xUnit** or **NUnit** to write unit tests for your repository implementations.

Example: Testing Product Repository

```csharp
Copy code
public class ProductRepositoryTests
{
    private readonly AppDbContext _context;
    private readonly ProductRepository _repository;

    public ProductRepositoryTests()
    {
        var options = new DbContextOptionsBuilder<AppDbContext>()
            .UseInMemoryDatabase(databaseName: "TestDatabase")
            .Options;

        _context = new AppDbContext(options);
        _repository = new ProductRepository(_context);
    }

    [Fact]
    public async Task GetProductById_ShouldReturnProduct_WhenExists()
    {
        var product = new Product("Test Product", 10.0m, 100);
        await _context.Products.AddAsync(product);
        await _context.SaveChangesAsync();

        var result = await _repository.GetProductById(product.Id);
        Assert.NotNull(result);
        Assert.Equal("Test Product", result.Name);
    }
}
```

Mocking External Services

For external service tests, you can use mocking frameworks like **Moq** to create test doubles for external dependencies.

Example: Mocking Payment Service in Tests

```csharp
Copy code
```

```csharp
public class CheckoutHandlerTests
{
    private readonly Mock<IPaymentService> _paymentServiceMock;
    private readonly CheckoutHandler _handler;

    public CheckoutHandlerTests()
    {
        _paymentServiceMock = new Mock<IPaymentService>();
        _handler = new CheckoutHandler(_paymentServiceMock.Object);
    }

    [Fact]
    public async Task Handle_ShouldProcessPayment_WhenValid()
    {
        _paymentServiceMock.Setup(x =>
        x.ProcessPayment(It.IsAny<decimal>(), It.IsAny<string>()))
            .ReturnsAsync(true);

        var command = new CheckoutCommand { Amount = 100,
        PaymentMethod = "CreditCard" };
        await _handler.Handle(command, CancellationToken.None);

        _paymentServiceMock.Verify(x => x.ProcessPayment(100,
        "CreditCard"), Times.Once);
    }
}
```

Section 7: Best Practices for the Infrastructure Layer

To ensure that the infrastructure layer remains clean and maintainable, follow these best practices:

1. **Keep It Separate**: Ensure that the infrastructure layer is distinct from the domain and application layers, adhering to the dependency rule.
2. **Follow the Interface Segregation Principle**: Define clear interfaces for repositories and services to avoid forcing implementations to expose unnecessary methods.

3. **Use Dependency Injection**: Utilize dependency injection for managing dependencies, making it easy to swap implementations for testing or during changes.
4. **Manage Configuration**: Keep configuration settings (like connection strings) outside of your codebase, using configuration files or environment variables instead.
5. **Implement Retry Logic**: For external service calls, implement retry logic for transient failures to improve resilience.
6. **Document Your Code**: Maintain clear documentation for your infrastructure components to help other developers understand the integration points and dependencies.

Conclusion

In this chapter, we explored the infrastructure layer of Clean Architecture in depth. We discussed the responsibilities of the infrastructure layer, how to set up data access with Entity Framework Core, implement repositories, integrate external services, and manage logging. We also highlighted the importance of testing and provided best practices to ensure that the infrastructure layer remains clean, maintainable, and aligned with the principles of Clean Architecture.

With a solid understanding of the infrastructure layer, you are now prepared to explore how to connect everything together in the presentation layer in the next chapter. This will involve exposing the application's functionality through APIs or user interfaces, ensuring that users can interact with your system effectively.

Chapter 6: Implementing the Presentation Layer in Clean Architecture

Introduction

The **Presentation Layer** is the outermost layer of Clean Architecture, responsible for interacting with users and presenting the data from the application layer. Whether it's a web application, an API, or a desktop application, the presentation layer plays a crucial role in ensuring a good user experience while maintaining a clean separation from the business logic.

In this chapter, you will learn:

- The role and responsibilities of the presentation layer.
- How to build a web API using ASP.NET Core.
- How to manage user interactions and data binding in a web application.
- Best practices for structuring the presentation layer.
- How to implement security measures, such as authentication and authorization.

By the end of this chapter, you will have a solid understanding of how to implement a robust presentation layer that interacts effectively with the application layer and adheres to Clean Architecture principles.

Section 1: Overview of the Presentation Layer

The presentation layer serves as the interface between the user and the application. Its primary responsibilities include:

1. **User Interface (UI) Management**: Displaying data to users and receiving user input.
2. **Data Binding**: Connecting the UI with the application layer to send and receive data.
3. **Interaction Handling**: Managing user interactions and events, such as button clicks and form submissions.
4. **Validation**: Ensuring that user inputs meet certain criteria before passing them to the application layer.
5. **Security Management**: Implementing authentication and authorization to protect resources.

Characteristics of the Presentation Layer

- **Decoupled from Business Logic**: The presentation layer should not contain business rules or logic; it simply interacts with the application layer.
- **User-Centric**: The design should focus on delivering a great user experience, with a responsive and intuitive interface.
- **Flexible and Scalable**: The layer should be structured to allow for changes in UI technology or design without affecting the underlying application logic.

Section 2: Building a Web API with ASP.NET Core

ASP.NET Core is a modern, high-performance framework for building web applications and APIs. In this section, we will walk through the steps of creating a web API that follows Clean Architecture principles.

Step 1: Creating a New ASP.NET Core Web API Project

CHAPTER 6: IMPLEMENTING THE PRESENTATION LAYER IN CLEAN...

To start building your API, create a new project in Visual Studio.

1. Open Visual Studio and select **Create a new project**.
2. Choose **ASP.NET Core Web API**.
3. Name your project (e.g., CleanArchitecture.WebAPI).
4. Select the target framework (.NET 6) and click **Create**.

Step 2: Configuring the API

Once your project is created, configure it to use the necessary services and middleware.

Example: Configuring Middleware in Program.cs

```csharp
Copy code
var builder = WebApplication.CreateBuilder(args);

// Add services to the container.
builder.Services.AddControllers();
builder.Services.AddEndpointsApiExplorer();
builder.Services.AddSwaggerGen();

// Register application services
builder.Services.AddScoped<IProductRepository, ProductRepository>();
builder.Services.AddScoped<IOrderRepository, OrderRepository>();
builder.Services.AddScoped<IPaymentService, PaymentService>();
builder.Services.AddMediatR(typeof(CreateOrderHandler).Assembly);

var app = builder.Build();

// Configure the HTTP request pipeline.
if (app.Environment.IsDevelopment())
{
    app.UseSwagger();
    app.UseSwaggerUI();
}
```

```
app.UseHttpsRedirection();
app.UseAuthorization();
app.MapControllers();
app.Run();
```

In this configuration, we have added services for dependency injection, enabled Swagger for API documentation, and configured HTTPS redirection and authorization.

Section 3: Implementing API Controllers

API controllers are the entry points for client requests. They handle incoming HTTP requests, process them, and return appropriate responses.

Step 1: Creating API Controllers

Create a new folder called **Controllers** in your web API project. Inside this folder, add a controller for your resources.

Example: Creating a ProductsController

```csharp
Copy code
[ApiController]
[Route("api/[controller]")]
public class ProductsController : ControllerBase
{
    private readonly IMediator _mediator;

    public ProductsController(IMediator mediator)
    {
        _mediator = mediator;
    }

    [HttpGet("{id}")]
    public async Task<ActionResult<ProductDto>> GetProductById(int id)
    {
        var query = new GetProductByIdQuery(id);
```

CHAPTER 6: IMPLEMENTING THE PRESENTATION LAYER IN CLEAN...

```csharp
    var product = await _mediator.Send(query);

    if (product == null)
        return NotFound();

    return Ok(product);
}

[HttpPost]
public async Task<ActionResult<int>> CreateProduct([FromBody]
CreateProductCommand command)
{
    var productId = await _mediator.Send(command);
    return CreatedAtAction(nameof(GetProductById), new { id =
    productId }, productId);
}
}
```

In this example, the ProductsController handles GET and POST requests for product resources. It uses MediatR to send commands and queries to the application layer, keeping the controller clean and focused on handling HTTP requests.

Step 2: Managing Responses and Errors

It's important to manage responses and errors effectively in your API. You can create custom error responses to standardize how errors are handled.

Example: Custom Error Response

```csharp
Copy code
public class ApiResponse<T>
{
    public T Data { get; set; }
    public string Message { get; set; }
    public bool Success { get; set; }

    public ApiResponse(T data, string message, bool success)
    {
```

```
        Data = data;
        Message = message;
        Success = success;
    }
}
```

Using Custom Responses in Controllers

```csharp
Copy code
[HttpGet("{id}")]
public async Task<ActionResult<ApiResponse<ProductDto>>> 
GetProductById(int id)
{
    var query = new GetProductByIdQuery(id);
    var product = await _mediator.Send(query);

    if (product == null)
        return NotFound(new ApiResponse<ProductDto>(null, "Product 
        not found", false));

    return Ok(new ApiResponse<ProductDto>(product, "Product 
    retrieved successfully", true));
}
```

Section 4: Securing the Presentation Layer

Security is a vital aspect of any application, especially in the presentation layer, where user data and interactions occur. This section covers authentication and authorization in ASP.NET Core.

Step 1: Adding Authentication

ASP.NET Core provides several authentication schemes, including JWT Bearer authentication for APIs. To implement JWT authentication, you need to install the relevant NuGet package.

```bash
Copy code
dotnet add package Microsoft.AspNetCore.Authentication.JwtBearer
```

Step 2: Configuring JWT Authentication

In your Program.cs, configure the JWT authentication middleware.

Example: Configuring JWT Authentication

```csharp
Copy code
builder.Services.AddAuthentication(options =>
{
    options.DefaultAuthenticateScheme =
    JwtBearerDefaults.AuthenticationScheme;
    options.DefaultChallengeScheme =
    JwtBearerDefaults.AuthenticationScheme;
}).AddJwtBearer(options =>
{
    options.TokenValidationParameters = new
    TokenValidationParameters
    {
        ValidateIssuer = true,
        ValidateAudience = true,
        ValidateLifetime = true,
        ValidateIssuerSigningKey = true,
        ValidIssuer = "YourIssuer",
        ValidAudience = "YourAudience",
        IssuerSigningKey = new
        SymmetricSecurityKey(Encoding.UTF8.GetBytes("YourSecretKey"))
    };
});
```

Step 3: Implementing Authorization Policies

You can create authorization policies to restrict access to certain endpoints.

Example: Defining an Authorization Policy

```csharp
Copy code
builder.Services.AddAuthorization(options =>
{
    options.AddPolicy("AdminOnly", policy =>
    policy.RequireRole("Admin"));
});
```

Using Authorization in Controllers

```csharp
Copy code
[Authorize(Policy = "AdminOnly")]
[HttpPost("admin")]
public async Task<IActionResult> CreateAdminProduct([FromBody] CreateProductCommand command)
{
    var productId = await _mediator.Send(command);
    return CreatedAtAction(nameof(GetProductById), new { id = productId }, productId);
}
```

Section 5: Client-Side Interactions

If your application includes a front-end interface (e.g., a web application using Blazor or Angular), you need to manage client-side interactions effectively.

Client-Side Frameworks

For web applications, you can choose from various client-side frameworks such as **Blazor**, **React**, or **Angular**. In this chapter, we'll briefly discuss how to integrate with a Blazor front end.

Setting Up Blazor

1. Create a new Blazor WebAssembly project.
2. Add HTTP client services to your Blazor project to interact with the API.

Example: Configuring HTTP Client in Blazor

```csharp
Copy code
builder.Services.AddHttpClient("Api", client =>
{
    client.BaseAddress = new Uri("https://localhost:5001/api/");
});
```

Managing API Calls

Use the HTTP client to make API calls from your Blazor components.

Example: Fetching Products in Blazor

```razor
Copy code
@page "/products"
@inject IHttpClientFactory HttpClientFactory

<h3>Products</h3>
<ul>
@foreach (var product in products)
{
    <li>@product.Name - @product.Price</li>
}
</ul>

@code {
    private ProductDto[] products;

    protected override async Task OnInitializedAsync()
    {
        var client = HttpClientFactory.CreateClient("Api");
        products = await
        client.GetFromJsonAsync<ProductDto[]>("products");
    }
}
```

Section 6: Best Practices for the Presentation Layer

To ensure that your presentation layer remains maintainable, user-friendly, and secure, consider the following best practices:

1. **Maintain Separation of Concerns**: Ensure that your presentation layer interacts only with the application layer. Avoid embedding business logic within controllers or views.
2. **Implement Validation**: Validate user inputs both client-side and server-side to enhance security and user experience.
3. **Utilize Dependency Injection**: Use dependency injection to manage dependencies within the presentation layer, making it easier to test and maintain.
4. **Follow RESTful Principles**: If building an API, follow RESTful conventions to create clear and understandable endpoints.
5. **Optimize Performance**: Utilize caching, minimize payload sizes, and use asynchronous calls to enhance performance.
6. **Implement Logging**: Log important events and errors to aid in debugging and monitoring application health.

Conclusion

In this chapter, we explored the presentation layer of Clean Architecture, focusing on how to build a web API using ASP.NET Core. We discussed the responsibilities of the presentation layer, how to implement API controllers, manage user interactions, and secure the application.

By following Clean Architecture principles, you ensure that your presentation layer is decoupled from business logic while providing a seamless user experience. In the next chapter, we will focus on testing strategies for Clean Architecture, exploring how to effectively test each layer of your application to ensure its reliability and performance.

Chapter 7: Testing Strategies for Clean Architecture

Introduction

Testing is a crucial aspect of software development, ensuring that your application behaves as expected and meets the requirements of the users. In the context of Clean Architecture, testing becomes even more critical due to the separation of concerns and the layering of components. Each layer of Clean Architecture presents unique challenges and opportunities for testing.

In this chapter, you will learn:

- The importance of testing in Clean Architecture.
- Different types of tests and their purposes.
- Strategies for unit testing domain entities, application services, and infrastructure components.
- Best practices for writing effective tests.
- How to implement automated testing in your CI/CD pipeline.

By the end of this chapter, you will have a thorough understanding of how to implement robust testing strategies for your Clean Architecture application.

Section 1: The Importance of Testing in Clean Architecture

Testing serves several essential purposes in software development:

1. **Ensuring Quality**: Tests help identify bugs and issues early in the development process, ensuring that your application functions as intended.
2. **Facilitating Refactoring**: With a comprehensive suite of tests, you can refactor code with confidence, knowing that existing functionality is covered.
3. **Enhancing Maintainability**: Well-tested code is easier to maintain and modify, as tests serve as documentation for how the system should behave.
4. **Supporting Agile Development**: Automated tests enable rapid iteration and deployment, supporting agile methodologies and continuous delivery.

In Clean Architecture, testing is essential due to the modular nature of the application. Each layer can be tested independently, allowing for focused testing strategies that ensure the integrity of the overall system.

Section 2: Types of Tests in Clean Architecture

There are several types of tests that can be employed in a Clean Architecture project. Each type serves a different purpose and focuses on different aspects of the application.

1. Unit Tests

Unit tests are designed to verify the behavior of individual components in isolation. They are typically written for functions, methods, or classes and ensure that they perform as expected given specific inputs.

Characteristics of Unit Tests:

- Fast to execute.

CHAPTER 7: TESTING STRATEGIES FOR CLEAN ARCHITECTURE

- Should not depend on external systems (like databases or web services).
- Focus on a single "unit" of code.

Example: Unit Testing a Domain Entity

```csharp
Copy code
public class ProductTests
{
    [Fact]
    public void CreatingProduct_WithValidData_ShouldCreateProduct()
    {
        var product = new Product("Test Product", 10.0m, 100);

        Assert.NotNull(product);
        Assert.Equal("Test Product", product.Name);
        Assert.Equal(10.0m, product.Price);
        Assert.Equal(100, product.StockQuantity);
    }

    [Fact]
    public void UpdatingPrice_WithValidPrice_ShouldUpdatePrice()
    {
        var product = new Product("Test Product", 10.0m, 100);
        product.UpdatePrice(15.0m);

        Assert.Equal(15.0m, product.Price);
    }
}
```

2. Integration Tests

Integration tests verify that different components of the application work together as expected. They often involve testing multiple layers or interacting with external systems like databases or APIs.

Characteristics of Integration Tests:

- Generally slower than unit tests due to external dependencies.
- Should cover multiple components and their interactions.

Example: Integration Testing a Repository

```csharp
public class ProductRepositoryTests :
IClassFixture<DatabaseFixture>
{
    private readonly AppDbContext _context;
    private readonly ProductRepository _repository;

    public ProductRepositoryTests(DatabaseFixture fixture)
    {
        _context = fixture.CreateContext();
        _repository = new ProductRepository(_context);
    }

    [Fact]
    public async Task
    GetProductById_ShouldReturnProduct_WhenExists()
    {
        var product = new Product("Test Product", 10.0m, 100);
        await _context.Products.AddAsync(product);
        await _context.SaveChangesAsync();

        var result = await _repository.GetProductById(product.Id);
        Assert.NotNull(result);
        Assert.Equal("Test Product", result.Name);
    }
}
```

3. Functional Tests

Functional tests evaluate the application from the end-user perspective, verifying that the application meets its functional requirements. These tests often involve the entire application stack and can include user interface interactions.

Characteristics of Functional Tests:

- Test the application as a whole.

CHAPTER 7: TESTING STRATEGIES FOR CLEAN ARCHITECTURE

- Can be automated using tools like Selenium or Cypress.

Example: Functional Testing an API Endpoint

```csharp
Copy code
public class ProductsApiTests :
IClassFixture<WebApplicationFactory<Startup>>
{
    private readonly HttpClient _client;

    public ProductsApiTests(WebApplicationFactory<Startup> factory)
    {
        _client = factory.CreateClient();
    }

    [Fact]
    public async Task GetProductById_ReturnsOk_WhenProductExists()
    {
        var response = await _client.GetAsync("/api/products/1");
        response.EnsureSuccessStatusCode();
        var product = await
        response.Content.ReadFromJsonAsync<ProductDto>();

        Assert.NotNull(product);
        Assert.Equal(1, product.Id);
    }
}
```

Section 3: Unit Testing the Domain Layer

The domain layer is critical to the application's business logic, making unit testing in this layer particularly important. In this section, we will focus on how to write effective unit tests for domain entities, value objects, and domain services.

1. Testing Domain Entities

Domain entities encapsulate business rules and behaviors. When testing these entities, you should focus on their methods and properties to ensure they work correctly.

Example: Testing a Product Entity

```csharp
Copy code
public class ProductTests
{
    [Fact]
    public void UpdatePrice_ValidPrice_ShouldUpdatePrice()
    {
        // Arrange
        var product = new Product("Sample Product", 20.0m, 10);

        // Act
        product.UpdatePrice(25.0m);

        // Assert
        Assert.Equal(25.0m, product.Price);
    }

    [Fact]
    public void ReduceStock_ValidQuantity_ShouldReduceStock()
    {
        // Arrange
        var product = new Product("Sample Product", 20.0m, 10);

        // Act
        product.ReduceStock(5);

        // Assert
        Assert.Equal(5, product.StockQuantity);
    }

    [Fact]
    public void ReduceStock_ExceedingQuantity_ShouldThrowException()
    {
        // Arrange
```

CHAPTER 7: TESTING STRATEGIES FOR CLEAN ARCHITECTURE

```csharp
        var product = new Product("Sample Product", 20.0m, 10);

        // Act & Assert
        Assert.Throws<InvalidOperationException>(() =>
        product.ReduceStock(15));
    }
}
```

2. Testing Value Objects

Value objects should also be tested, especially for their equality and behavior.

Example: Testing a Money Value Object

```csharp
Copy code
public class MoneyTests
{
    [Fact]
    public void Equals_ShouldReturnTrue_ForEqualValueObjects()
    {
        var money1 = new Money(10, "USD");
        var money2 = new Money(10, "USD");

        Assert.True(money1.Equals(money2));
    }

    [Fact]
    public void Add_ShouldReturnNewMoneyObject()
    {
        var money1 = new Money(10, "USD");
        var money2 = new Money(5, "USD");

        var result = money1.Add(money2);

        Assert.Equal(15, result.Amount);
    }

    [Fact]
```

```csharp
    public void Add_DifferentCurrencies_ShouldThrowException()
    {
        var money1 = new Money(10, "USD");
        var money2 = new Money(5, "EUR");

        Assert.Throws<InvalidOperationException>(() =>
        money1.Add(money2));
    }
}
```

3. Testing Domain Services

Domain services that encapsulate complex business logic should also be thoroughly tested.

Example: Testing a Shipping Service

```csharp
Copy code
public class ShippingServiceTests
{
    [Fact]
    public void CalculateShippingCost_OrderUnder100_ShouldReturnBaseCost()
    {
        var service = new ShippingService();
        var order = new Order { TotalAmount = 80 };

        var cost = service.CalculateShippingCost(order);

        Assert.Equal(10, cost);
    }

    [Fact]
    public void CalculateShippingCost_OrderOver100_ShouldReturnZero()
    {
        var service = new ShippingService();
        var order = new Order { TotalAmount = 120 };
```

```csharp
        var cost = service.CalculateShippingCost(order);

        Assert.Equal(0, cost);
    }
}
```

Section 4: Integration Testing the Application Layer

Integration tests validate that the application layer works correctly with the domain and infrastructure layers. This section will focus on how to set up and execute integration tests effectively.

1. Setting Up the Integration Testing Environment

When writing integration tests, it's important to isolate your test environment to ensure tests do not interfere with each other. Using an in-memory database is a common approach.

Example: Creating an In-Memory Database Fixture

```csharp
Copy code
public class DatabaseFixture : IDisposable
{
    public AppDbContext CreateContext()
    {
        var options = new DbContextOptionsBuilder<AppDbContext>()
            .UseInMemoryDatabase(databaseName:
            Guid.NewGuid().ToString())
            .Options;

        var context = new AppDbContext(options);
        context.Database.EnsureCreated();
        return context;
    }

    public void Dispose()
    {
```

        // Clean up resources
    }
}

2. Integration Testing Repositories and Services

Integration tests for repositories should ensure that data is correctly stored and retrieved from the database.

Example: Integration Testing the Product Repository

```csharp
Copy code
public class ProductRepositoryIntegrationTests :
IClassFixture<DatabaseFixture>
{
    private readonly AppDbContext _context;
    private readonly ProductRepository _repository;

    public ProductRepositoryIntegrationTests(DatabaseFixture fixture)
    {
        _context = fixture.CreateContext();
        _repository = new ProductRepository(_context);
    }

    [Fact]
    public async Task AddAsync_ShouldPersistProduct()
    {
        var product = new Product("New Product", 15.0m, 50);
        await _repository.AddAsync(product);

        var result = await _repository.GetProductById(product.Id);
        Assert.NotNull(result);
        Assert.Equal("New Product", result.Name);
    }
}
```

3. Integration Testing Application Services

When testing application services, ensure that the entire flow of data is validated. This includes verifying that commands result in the expected state in the database.

Example: Integration Testing CheckoutHandler

```csharp
Copy code
public class CheckoutHandlerIntegrationTests : IClassFixture<DatabaseFixture>
{
    private readonly CheckoutHandler _handler;
    private readonly IOrderRepository _orderRepository;
    private readonly IProductRepository _productRepository;

    public CheckoutHandlerIntegrationTests(DatabaseFixture fixture)
    {
        var context = fixture.CreateContext();
        _productRepository = new ProductRepository(context);
        _orderRepository = new OrderRepository(context);
        _handler = new CheckoutHandler(_orderRepository, _productRepository);
    }

    [Fact]
    public async Task Handle_ShouldCreateOrder_WhenValid()
    {
        var product = new Product("Sample Product", 10.0m, 100);
        await _productRepository.AddAsync(product);

        var command = new CheckoutCommand { ProductId = product.Id, Quantity = 1 };
        await _handler.Handle(command, CancellationToken.None);

        var order = await _orderRepository.GetByIdAsync(1);
        Assert.NotNull(order);
        Assert.Single(order.Items);
    }
}
```

Section 5: Functional Testing the Presentation Layer

Functional tests evaluate the application from an end-user perspective, ensuring that the user interface and API behave as expected. This section focuses on how to set up and execute functional tests.

1. Setting Up Functional Testing Frameworks

For functional testing of web APIs, you can use **Selenium**, **Cypress**, or the built-in test server with **ASP.NET Core**.

Example: Using the ASP.NET Core Test Host

```csharp
csharp
Copy code
public class ProductsApiTests : IClassFixture<WebApplicationFactory<Startup>>
{
    private readonly HttpClient _client;

    public ProductsApiTests(WebApplicationFactory<Startup> factory)
    {
        _client = factory.CreateClient();
    }

    [Fact]
    public async Task CreateProduct_ShouldReturnCreated_WhenValid()
    {
        var product = new CreateProductCommand { Name = "Test Product", Price = 10.0m, StockQuantity = 50 };

        var response = await _client.PostAsJsonAsync("/api/products", product);

        response.EnsureSuccessStatusCode();
        var createdProductId = await response.Content.ReadAsAsync<int>();

        Assert.True(createdProductId > 0);
    }
}
```

2. Functional Testing API Endpoints

Functional tests should cover all API endpoints to ensure they return the expected results for various inputs.

Example: Testing Get Product Endpoint

```csharp
Copy code
[Fact]
public async Task GetProductById_ShouldReturnOk_WhenProductExists()
{
    var response = await _client.GetAsync("/api/products/1");
    response.EnsureSuccessStatusCode();

    var product = await response.Content.ReadFromJsonAsync<ProductDto>();
    Assert.NotNull(product);
    Assert.Equal(1, product.Id);
}
```

3. Testing User Interface Interactions

If your application includes a front-end UI, testing user interactions is critical. Use frameworks like **Selenium** or **Cypress** to automate browser interactions.

Example: Testing a Blazor Component

```csharp
Copy code
public class ProductComponentTests : ComponentTestFixture
{
    [Fact]
    public async Task RenderProductList_ShouldDisplayProducts()
    {
        var products = new List<ProductDto>
        {
            new ProductDto { Id = 1, Name = "Product 1", Price = 10 },
            new ProductDto { Id = 2, Name = "Product 2", Price = 20 }
```

```csharp
        };

        var component = RenderComponent<ProductList>(parameters =>
        parameters.Add(p => p.Products, products));

        var productElements = component.FindAll("li");
        Assert.Equal(2, productElements.Count);
    }
}
```

Section 6: Best Practices for Testing in Clean Architecture

To ensure that your testing strategy is effective, follow these best practices:

1. **Write Tests Early**: Adopt a test-driven development (TDD) approach where you write tests before implementing functionality.
2. **Keep Tests Isolated**: Each test should be independent of others. Use mocking frameworks to isolate dependencies and control the environment.
3. **Use Meaningful Names**: Name your tests descriptively to convey their purpose and expected behavior.
4. **Organize Tests**: Structure your tests in a way that mirrors your application structure, making it easy to find and manage tests.
5. **Automate Tests**: Use a CI/CD pipeline to run tests automatically on code changes, ensuring that new changes do not introduce regressions.
6. **Test Coverage**: Aim for high test coverage but focus on critical areas that impact business logic and functionality.
7. **Review and Refactor**: Regularly review your tests to ensure they remain relevant and effective as your application evolves.

CHAPTER 7: TESTING STRATEGIES FOR CLEAN ARCHITECTURE

Conclusion

In this chapter, we explored various testing strategies applicable to Clean Architecture. We covered unit testing for domain entities and application services, integration testing for repositories and services, and functional testing for APIs and user interfaces. Each type of test serves a unique purpose in ensuring the reliability and performance of your application.

By implementing a comprehensive testing strategy, you ensure that your Clean Architecture application is robust, maintainable, and capable of evolving with changing requirements. In the next chapter, we will focus on deployment strategies and best practices for deploying Clean Architecture applications to production environments.

Chapter 8: Deployment Strategies for Clean Architecture

Introduction

Deploying applications can often be one of the most complex aspects of software development. In Clean Architecture, the deployment strategy must consider the structure of the application, the technologies used, and the target environment. Effective deployment practices are essential for ensuring that your application performs well, remains secure, and can be updated with minimal downtime.

In this chapter, you will learn:
- Various deployment options for Clean Architecture applications.
- How to set up CI/CD pipelines for automation.
- Best practices for deploying and managing .NET applications in production.
- Strategies for monitoring and maintaining application health post-deployment.

By the end of this chapter, you will have a solid understanding of how to deploy your Clean Architecture application and ensure its longevity in production.

CHAPTER 8: DEPLOYMENT STRATEGIES FOR CLEAN ARCHITECTURE

Section 1: Overview of Deployment Options

Deployment refers to the process of making an application available for use. There are various deployment options available, depending on the application's architecture, the infrastructure, and the operational requirements.

1. On-Premises Deployment

On-premises deployment involves hosting the application on servers that are physically located within the organization's premises. This option provides full control over the hardware and software stack but requires a dedicated IT team for maintenance and management.

Pros:

- Full control over infrastructure.
- Customizable configurations and environments.
- Potentially lower long-term costs for large-scale operations.

Cons:

- High upfront costs for hardware and licensing.
- Ongoing maintenance and support responsibilities.
- Longer time to scale.

2. Cloud Deployment

Cloud deployment involves hosting applications on cloud service providers like Microsoft Azure, Amazon Web Services (AWS), or Google Cloud Platform (GCP). This option offers scalability, flexibility, and reduced operational overhead.

Pros:

- Easy to scale resources up or down based on demand.
- Lower upfront costs; pay-as-you-go pricing models.
- Reduced need for in-house infrastructure management.

Cons:

- Ongoing costs can increase depending on usage.
- Dependency on third-party providers for uptime and performance.
- Potential data security concerns.

3. Hybrid Deployment

Hybrid deployment combines on-premises and cloud environments, allowing organizations to leverage the benefits of both. Sensitive data can remain on-premises while using the cloud for less sensitive workloads.

Pros:

- Flexibility to use both environments as needed.
- Control over sensitive data and compliance requirements.
- Ability to scale cloud resources while retaining local control.

Cons:

- Complexity in managing multiple environments.
- Potential integration challenges between on-premises and cloud systems.
- Requires skilled personnel for maintenance.

Section 2: Preparing Your Application for Deployment

Before deploying your application, it's essential to prepare it for the target environment. This includes ensuring that it's built correctly, dependencies are managed, and configurations are set.

1. Configuration Management

Configuration management involves handling settings that vary between environments (development, staging, production). In .NET, this is typically done using appsettings.json files or environment variables.

Example: Using appsettings.json

CHAPTER 8: DEPLOYMENT STRATEGIES FOR CLEAN ARCHITECTURE

```json
Copy code
{
  "ConnectionStrings": {
    "DefaultConnection": "Server=localhost;Database=MyApp;User Id=myuser;Password=mypassword;"
  },
  "Logging": {
    "LogLevel": {
      "Default": "Information"
    }
  }
}
```

2. Build Configuration

Building your application for deployment is crucial. Ensure that your project is configured for the correct build environment.

Example: Building for Production

```bash
Copy code
dotnet publish -c Release -o ./publish
```

This command compiles the application and prepares it for deployment in the specified output directory.

3. Managing Secrets

Sensitive information, such as API keys and database connection strings, should not be hard-coded. Use secure secret management tools like Azure Key Vault, AWS Secrets Manager, or environment variables.

Section 3: Continuous Integration and Continuous Deployment (CI/CD)

CI/CD is a set of practices that enable development teams to deliver code changes more frequently and reliably. Setting up a CI/CD pipeline automates the process of testing and deploying your application.

1. Setting Up CI/CD Pipelines

A CI/CD pipeline consists of stages such as build, test, and deploy. Various tools can be used to implement CI/CD, including Azure DevOps, GitHub Actions, Jenkins, and CircleCI.

Example: Setting Up a CI/CD Pipeline with GitHub Actions

1. **Create a GitHub Actions Workflow**:

- In your GitHub repository, create a new directory called .github/workflows.
- Create a file named ci-cd.yml and define your pipeline.

```yaml
Copy code
name: CI/CD Pipeline

on:
  push:
    branches:
      - main

jobs:
  build:
    runs-on: ubuntu-latest
    steps:
      - name: Checkout Code
        uses: actions/checkout@v2
```

CHAPTER 8: DEPLOYMENT STRATEGIES FOR CLEAN ARCHITECTURE

```yaml
    - name: Setup .NET
      uses: actions/setup-dotnet@v1
      with:
        dotnet-version: '6.0.x'

    - name: Restore Dependencies
      run: dotnet restore

    - name: Build Application
      run: dotnet build --configuration Release

    - name: Run Tests
      run: dotnet test --configuration Release

    - name: Publish
      run: dotnet publish --configuration Release --output
        ./publish

deploy:
  runs-on: ubuntu-latest
  needs: build
  steps:
    - name: Deploy to Azure
      uses: Azure/webapps-deploy@v2
      with:
        app-name: 'YourAppName'
        slot-name: 'production'
        publish-profile: ${{
          secrets.AZURE_WEBAPP_PUBLISH_PROFILE }}
        package: './publish'
```

2. Automated Testing in CI/CD

Integrate automated tests into your CI/CD pipeline. Ensure that your tests run every time code is pushed or a pull request is created.

Example: Adding Testing to CI/CD

Include the testing commands in your CI/CD workflow as shown in the example above. This ensures that any broken tests prevent deployment, maintaining code quality.

3. Monitoring CI/CD Performance

Monitoring the performance of your CI/CD pipeline is crucial for identifying bottlenecks and optimizing the build and deployment process. Use tools and dashboards provided by your CI/CD platform to track build times, success rates, and test results.

Section 4: Deployment Strategies for Production

Once your application is prepared and your CI/CD pipeline is in place, it's time to consider how to deploy it to production. Various strategies can be employed depending on your application's requirements and infrastructure.

1. Blue-Green Deployment

Blue-Green Deployment involves having two identical environments: one active (blue) and one standby (green). The new version of the application is deployed to the inactive environment. After testing, traffic is switched to the new version.

Pros:

- Minimal downtime during deployment.
- Easy rollback to the previous version if issues arise.

Cons:

- Requires double the resources for two environments.
- Potential complexity in managing environment configurations.

2. Canary Releases

Canary Releases involve deploying the new version to a small subset of users before rolling it out to the entire user base. This allows you to monitor the new version's performance and catch issues early.

Pros:

- Reduces the risk of widespread failures.
- Provides real user feedback before full deployment.

Cons:

- Requires sophisticated traffic management.
- May complicate user experience if not managed well.

3. Rolling Deployment

Rolling Deployment gradually replaces instances of the previous version of the application with the new version. This method allows you to roll out updates without downtime.

Pros:

- Continuous availability of the application.
- Allows for gradual monitoring and validation of the new version.

Cons:

- More complex to set up and manage.
- Requires careful orchestration to avoid performance degradation.

Section 5: Monitoring and Maintenance

After deploying your application, ongoing monitoring and maintenance are essential to ensure optimal performance and reliability.

1. Application Monitoring

Use application performance monitoring (APM) tools to track the health and performance of your application. These tools can help identify issues such as slow response times, high error rates, and bottlenecks.

Popular APM Tools

- **Application Insights**: A Microsoft service for monitoring applications.
- **New Relic**: A cloud-based observability platform.
- **Datadog**: A monitoring and analytics platform for developers.

2. Logging for Diagnostics

Implement logging to capture application behavior and errors. Ensure that logs are structured and include essential context to aid in troubleshooting.

Example: Using Serilog for Logging

```bash
Copy code
dotnet add package Serilog.AspNetCore
dotnet add package Serilog.Sinks.Console
```

Configure Serilog in Program.cs

```csharp
Copy code
Log.Logger = new LoggerConfiguration()
    .MinimumLevel.Debug()
    .WriteTo.Console()
    .CreateLogger();

builder.Host.UseSerilog();
```

3. Health Checks

Implement health checks to monitor the status of your application and its dependencies (e.g., database connections, external APIs).

Example: Configuring Health Checks in ASP.NET Core

```csharp
Copy code
builder.Services.AddHealthChecks()
    .AddDbContextCheck<AppDbContext>("Database")
    .AddCheck<ExternalServiceHealthCheck>("External Service");
```

Section 6: Rollback Strategies

Having a rollback strategy is crucial in case of deployment failures. Ensure that you can quickly revert to a previous version without significant downtime.

1. Versioning and Backups

Maintain versioning for your deployments and ensure that backups are taken before each deployment. This allows you to restore the previous version if needed.

2. Database Rollbacks

In cases where the deployment involves database changes, ensure that you can rollback database migrations if necessary. Tools like Entity Framework Core support database migrations and can help manage schema changes.

Conclusion

In this chapter, we explored deployment strategies for Clean Architecture applications, including on-premises, cloud, and hybrid deployments. We discussed how to prepare your application for deployment, set up CI/CD pipelines for automation, and implement various deployment strategies.

We also covered the importance of monitoring and maintenance in production, ensuring that your application remains reliable and performant. With a solid understanding of deployment strategies, you are now equipped to deploy your Clean Architecture application effectively.

In the next chapter, we will explore advanced topics such as scaling your application, handling high traffic, and optimizing performance in a Clean Architecture context.

Chapter 9: Scaling and Performance Optimization in Clean Architecture

Introduction

In today's fast-paced digital landscape, applications must not only function correctly but also scale effectively to handle varying workloads. Clean Architecture provides a solid foundation for building applications, but scaling and optimizing performance requires additional considerations and strategies. This chapter will explore methods for scaling your application, optimizing its performance, and ensuring that it can handle increased traffic while maintaining a seamless user experience.

In this chapter, you will learn about:
- Understanding scalability and its importance.
- Different types of scaling: vertical vs. horizontal.
- Techniques for optimizing performance at various layers.
- Caching strategies to improve response times.
- Load balancing and its role in application scalability.
- Monitoring and analyzing application performance.

By the end of this chapter, you will have a clear understanding of how to implement scaling strategies and optimize performance for your Clean Architecture application.

Section 1: Understanding Scalability

Scalability refers to the capability of an application to handle increased loads without sacrificing performance. As user demands grow, your application must be able to adapt to accommodate this growth. Understanding the types of scalability is crucial for designing applications that can efficiently handle traffic spikes.

1. Types of Scalability

- **Vertical Scalability (Scaling Up)**: This involves adding more resources (CPU, memory) to a single server. While vertical scaling is often simpler, it has limitations and can lead to downtime during upgrades.
- **Horizontal Scalability (Scaling Out)**: This involves adding more servers to distribute the load. Horizontal scaling is more complex but provides better resilience and redundancy. It allows applications to handle larger traffic volumes by spreading requests across multiple servers.

2. Factors Affecting Scalability

- **Architecture**: The design of the application impacts how well it can scale. Clean Architecture naturally supports scalability due to its separation of concerns.
- **Data Management**: How data is stored and accessed can affect performance. Optimizing database queries and implementing caching can significantly enhance scalability.
- **Load Patterns**: Understanding user behavior and traffic patterns helps in planning for scalability. For instance, applications that experience seasonal traffic spikes may need different strategies compared to those with steady loads.

Section 2: Scaling Strategies for Clean Architecture Applications

Scaling your Clean Architecture application involves implementing strategies that allow it to grow seamlessly. Below are some effective strategies to consider.

1. Database Scaling

Databases are often the bottleneck in applications, so optimizing their performance is critical. Strategies for database scaling include:

- **Read Replicas**: Use read replicas to offload read operations from the primary database. This allows you to distribute read traffic and improve response times.
- **Sharding**: Split your database into smaller, more manageable pieces (shards) based on certain criteria (e.g., user ID). Each shard can be hosted on a separate server, distributing the load.
- **Caching**: Implement caching strategies to reduce the number of database queries. By storing frequently accessed data in memory, you can significantly improve performance.

Example: Setting Up Read Replicas in SQL Server You can configure SQL Server to create read replicas by setting up database mirroring or Always On availability groups. This allows you to direct read traffic to replicas while keeping write operations on the primary database.

2. API Scaling

As your application grows, the number of API calls may increase. Here are some strategies to scale your API:

- **Load Balancing**: Distribute incoming API requests across multiple servers using a load balancer. This helps ensure that no single server becomes a bottleneck.
- **Rate Limiting**: Implement rate limiting to control the number of requests from users. This prevents abuse and protects your services from being overwhelmed.

- **Asynchronous Processing**: Use background processing to handle long-running tasks. By offloading these tasks, you can keep your API responsive for users.

Example: Implementing Load Balancing with Nginx You can set up Nginx as a reverse proxy to distribute incoming API requests to multiple instances of your application.

```nginx
Copy code
http {
    upstream app_servers {
        server app_server_1;
        server app_server_2;
    }

    server {
        listen 80;

        location / {
            proxy_pass http://app_servers;
        }
    }
}
```

Section 3: Performance Optimization Techniques

Optimizing performance is crucial to providing a seamless user experience. This section covers various techniques to enhance the performance of your Clean Architecture application.

1. Code Optimization

Review your application code to identify and eliminate inefficiencies. This includes:

- **Avoiding Unnecessary Computation**: Ensure that computations

are done only when necessary. Cache results when possible to avoid recalculating.
- **Optimizing Algorithms**: Use efficient algorithms and data structures to improve performance. For example, replacing a linear search with a binary search can significantly reduce execution time.
- **Reducing Object Allocation**: Minimize memory allocation in performance-critical code paths. Reuse objects when possible to reduce garbage collection overhead.

2. Caching Strategies

Caching is one of the most effective ways to improve performance. By storing frequently accessed data in memory, you can reduce the load on your database and decrease response times.

Types of Caching

- **In-Memory Caching**: Store data in the application's memory for quick access. In .NET, you can use libraries like **MemoryCache** or **IMemoryCache**.
- **Distributed Caching**: For applications running on multiple servers, use a distributed cache like **Redis** or **Memcached**. This allows all instances to share cached data.

Example: Implementing In-Memory Caching in ASP.NET Core

```csharp
Copy code
public class Startup
{
    public void ConfigureServices(IServiceCollection services)
    {
        services.AddMemoryCache();
    }
}
```

CHAPTER 9: SCALING AND PERFORMANCE OPTIMIZATION IN CLEAN...

```csharp
public class ProductService
{
    private readonly IMemoryCache _cache;

    public ProductService(IMemoryCache cache)
    {
        _cache = cache;
    }

    public async Task<ProductDto> GetProductById(int id)
    {
        if (!_cache.TryGetValue(id, out ProductDto product))
        {
            product = await _repository.GetProductById(id);
            _cache.Set(id, product, TimeSpan.FromMinutes(5)); // Set cache expiration
        }
        return product;
    }
}
```

3. Asynchronous Programming

Utilizing asynchronous programming can significantly improve the responsiveness of your application. In .NET, the async and await keywords make it easy to perform non-blocking operations.

Example: Asynchronous Database Calls

csharp
Copy code
```
public async Task<ProductDto> GetProductByIdAsync(int id)
{
    var product = await _context.Products.FindAsync(id);
    return _mapper.Map<ProductDto>(product);
}
```

Section 4: Load Balancing Strategies

Load balancing distributes incoming network traffic across multiple servers, ensuring that no single server becomes overwhelmed. This section explores various load balancing techniques and strategies.

1. Round Robin Load Balancing

This is the simplest method of distributing requests. Incoming requests are sent to each server in a circular order.

Pros:

- Simple to implement.
- Effective when all servers have roughly equal capabilities.

Cons:

- May not account for varying server loads.

2. Least Connections Load Balancing

This method sends requests to the server with the fewest active connections. It is useful when server performance can vary.

Pros:

- Better suited for environments where server load varies significantly.

Cons:

- Slightly more complex than round-robin.

3. IP Hash Load Balancing

This method routes requests based on the hash of the client's IP address, ensuring that the same client always goes to the same server.

Pros:

CHAPTER 9: SCALING AND PERFORMANCE OPTIMIZATION IN CLEAN...

- Provides session persistence for users.

Cons:

- Imbalance can occur if certain IPs generate more requests.

Section 5: Monitoring Application Performance

Monitoring the performance of your application is critical for identifying bottlenecks and ensuring that the application remains responsive under load. This section discusses tools and techniques for monitoring application performance.

1. Application Performance Monitoring (APM) Tools

APM tools help track application performance in real-time. They provide insights into response times, error rates, and transaction traces.

Popular APM Tools

- **Application Insights**: A Microsoft service for monitoring applications hosted on Azure and on-premises.
- **New Relic**: A comprehensive monitoring solution for applications, servers, and infrastructure.
- **Datadog**: A monitoring and analytics platform for applications, databases, and servers.

2. Logging for Performance Insights

Implement structured logging to capture application events, errors, and performance metrics. Use logging frameworks like **Serilog**, **NLog**, or **Log4Net**.

Example: Structured Logging with Serilog

```
csharp
Copy code
```

```
Log.Logger = new LoggerConfiguration()
    .WriteTo.Console()
    .WriteTo.File("logs/log.txt", rollingInterval:
    RollingInterval.Day)
    .CreateLogger();

app.UseSerilogRequestLogging(); // Log HTTP requests
```

3. Performance Metrics

Define key performance indicators (KPIs) to monitor, such as:

- Response time.
- Error rates.
- System resource usage (CPU, memory).
- Database query performance.

Use tools like **Grafana** or **Prometheus** to visualize and analyze metrics over time.

Section 6: Handling Traffic Spikes and Load Testing

Preparing for traffic spikes and ensuring that your application can handle increased loads is crucial for maintaining performance.

1. Load Testing

Load testing simulates high traffic to identify how your application behaves under stress. This allows you to identify bottlenecks before they become real problems.

Popular Load Testing Tools:

- **Apache JMeter**: An open-source load testing tool that simulates multiple users.
- **k6**: A modern load testing tool built for developers.
- **Gatling**: A powerful load testing tool that focuses on ease of use.

2. Stress Testing

Stress testing goes beyond normal load testing to see how the system behaves under extreme conditions. It helps identify breaking points and resource exhaustion.

3. Auto-Scaling

Implement auto-scaling to dynamically adjust resources based on current demand. Many cloud providers offer auto-scaling capabilities that can automatically increase or decrease the number of active servers based on traffic patterns.

Example: Setting Up Auto-Scaling in Azure You can configure auto-scaling rules in Azure App Service based on CPU usage, memory, or HTTP requests.

Conclusion

In this chapter, we explored the critical topics of scaling and performance optimization for Clean Architecture applications. We discussed various scaling strategies, performance optimization techniques, load balancing, and the importance of monitoring application performance.

By implementing these strategies, you can ensure that your Clean Architecture application is capable of handling increased loads while maintaining optimal performance. In the next chapter, we will delve into advanced topics such as security considerations and implementing best practices for securing your application in production.

Chapter 10: Security Considerations and Best Practices in Clean Architecture

Introduction

In today's digital landscape, security is paramount. Applications are constantly targeted by malicious actors, and ensuring the integrity, confidentiality, and availability of your application is critical. In Clean Architecture, security must be considered at every layer, from the presentation layer down to the data layer.

In this chapter, you will learn about:
- The importance of security in application development.
- Best practices for implementing authentication and authorization.
- Strategies for protecting sensitive data.
- Common security vulnerabilities and how to mitigate them.
- Tools and techniques for securing your Clean Architecture applications.

By the end of this chapter, you will have a solid understanding of how to implement robust security measures throughout your Clean Architecture application.

CHAPTER 10: SECURITY CONSIDERATIONS AND BEST PRACTICES IN...

Section 1: The Importance of Security in Application Development

Security is a critical aspect of software development that ensures applications are protected against unauthorized access, data breaches, and other threats. The increasing prevalence of cyberattacks highlights the need for secure coding practices and robust security measures.

1. Understanding Security Risks

Common security risks that applications face include:

- **Data Breaches**: Unauthorized access to sensitive data can lead to significant financial and reputational damage.
- **Injection Attacks**: Attacks such as SQL injection exploit vulnerabilities in applications to manipulate data.
- **Cross-Site Scripting (XSS)**: Malicious scripts are injected into web pages, compromising user data and sessions.
- **Cross-Site Request Forgery (CSRF)**: Unauthorized commands are transmitted from a user that the web application trusts.

2. The Security Lifecycle

Implementing security is not a one-time task; it is an ongoing process that spans the entire application lifecycle. Security should be integrated into the design, development, testing, deployment, and maintenance phases of your application.

Section 2: Authentication and Authorization Best Practices

Authentication and authorization are critical components of application security, determining who can access your application and what actions they can perform.

1. Understanding Authentication vs. Authorization

- **Authentication**: The process of verifying the identity of a user or service. Common methods include username/password combinations, OAuth

tokens, and biometric methods.
- **Authorization**: The process of determining whether an authenticated user has permission to access specific resources or perform actions.

2. Implementing Secure Authentication

Secure authentication mechanisms protect user credentials and ensure that only authorized users can access your application.

Best Practices for Authentication:

- **Use Strong Password Policies**: Require users to create complex passwords and implement password strength checks.
- **Multi-Factor Authentication (MFA)**: Enhance security by requiring additional verification methods, such as SMS codes or authentication apps.
- **Secure Password Storage**: Use hashing algorithms (e.g., bcrypt, PBKDF2) to securely store user passwords in your database.

Example: Using ASP.NET Core Identity for Authentication ASP.NET Core Identity provides a robust framework for managing user authentication.

1. **Install the ASP.NET Core Identity package**:

```bash
Copy code
dotnet add package Microsoft.AspNetCore.Identity
```

1. **Configure Identity in Startup.cs**:

CHAPTER 10: SECURITY CONSIDERATIONS AND BEST PRACTICES IN...

```csharp
Copy code
public void ConfigureServices(IServiceCollection services)
{
    services.AddDbContext<
ApplicationDbContext>(options =>
        options.UseSqlServer(Configuration.
GetConnectionString("DefaultConnection")));

    services.AddIdentity
<ApplicationUser, IdentityRole>()
        .AddEntityFrameworkStores
<ApplicationDbContext>()
        .AddDefaultTokenProviders();
}
```

1. **Create a User Registration Endpoint**:

```csharp
Copy code
[HttpPost("register")]
public async Task<IActionResult> Register([FromBody] RegisterDto registerDto)
{
    var user = new ApplicationUser { UserName = registerDto.Email, Email = registerDto.Email };
    var result = await _userManager.CreateAsync(user, registerDto.Password);

    if (!result.Succeeded)
        return BadRequest(result.Errors);

    return Ok();
}
```

3. Implementing Authorization

Authorization ensures that users have the necessary permissions to access specific resources.

Best Practices for Authorization:

- **Role-Based Access Control (RBAC)**: Use roles to group users and assign permissions based on their role.
- **Claims-Based Authorization**: Use claims to provide fine-grained access control based on user attributes.

Example: Implementing Role-Based Authorization in ASP.NET Core

```csharp
Copy code
[Authorize(Roles = "Admin")]
[HttpPost("admin")]
public IActionResult AdminAction()
{
    return Ok("This action is restricted to Admins.");
}
```

Section 3: Protecting Sensitive Data

Sensitive data, such as user credentials, financial information, and personal data, must be protected to prevent unauthorized access and breaches.

1. Data Encryption

Encrypt sensitive data both at rest (stored data) and in transit (data being transmitted over networks) to protect it from unauthorized access.

Best Practices for Encryption:

- **Use HTTPS**: Always encrypt data in transit by using HTTPS for your web applications. This protects against eavesdropping and man-in-the-middle attacks.
- **Encrypt Sensitive Data in the Database**: Use encryption for sensitive fields in your database, such as credit card numbers and personal identification numbers.

CHAPTER 10: SECURITY CONSIDERATIONS AND BEST PRACTICES IN...

Example: Encrypting Data in .NET Core You can use the Aes encryption class to encrypt sensitive data.

```csharp
Copy code
public static string EncryptString(string plainText, string key)
{
    using (Aes aes = Aes.Create())
    {
        // Set key and initialization vector
        aes.Key = Encoding.UTF8.GetBytes(key);
        aes.IV = new byte[16];
// Initialization vector (IV)

        ICryptoTransform encryptor = aes.CreateEncryptor(aes.Key, aes.IV);

        using (MemoryStream ms = new MemoryStream())
        {
            using (CryptoStream cs = new CryptoStream(ms, encryptor, CryptoStreamMode.Write))
            {
                using (StreamWriter sw = new StreamWriter(cs))
                {
                    sw.Write(plainText);
                }
                return Convert.ToBase64String(ms.ToArray());
            }
        }
    }
}
```

2. Data Minimization

Limit the collection and storage of sensitive data to only what is necessary for your application. This reduces the risk associated with data breaches.

Section 4: Common Vulnerabilities and Mitigations

Understanding common security vulnerabilities helps you design more secure applications. This section discusses several common vulnerabilities and strategies to mitigate them.

1. SQL Injection

SQL injection occurs when an attacker is able to execute arbitrary SQL queries against your database by manipulating user input.

Mitigation Strategies:

- **Use Parameterized Queries**: Always use parameterized queries or prepared statements to safely handle user input.
- **Use ORM Tools**: Utilize Object-Relational Mapping (ORM) tools like Entity Framework, which automatically parameterizes queries.

2. Cross-Site Scripting (XSS)

XSS attacks occur when attackers inject malicious scripts into web pages viewed by users.

Mitigation Strategies:

- **Sanitize User Input**: Always sanitize and validate user input to prevent malicious code from being executed.
- **Use Content Security Policy (CSP)**: Implement CSP headers to restrict sources of executable scripts.

Example: Configuring CSP in ASP.NET Core

```csharp
Copy code
app.Use(async (context, next) =>
{
    context.Response.Headers.Add("Content-Security-Policy",
    "default-src 'self'");
```

```
    await next();
});
```

3. Cross-Site Request Forgery (CSRF)

CSRF attacks force a user to execute unwanted actions on a web application where they are authenticated.

Mitigation Strategies:

- **Use Anti-CSRF Tokens**: Implement anti-CSRF tokens that validate requests made by users.

Example: Implementing Anti-CSRF Tokens in ASP.NET Core

```csharp
Copy code
services.AddAntiforgery(options =>
  options.HeaderName = "X-CSRF-TOKEN");
```

Section 5: Tools and Techniques for Securing Clean Architecture Applications

Implementing security requires a combination of tools and techniques. This section covers various tools that can help enhance the security of your Clean Architecture applications.

1. Security Testing Tools

Use automated security testing tools to scan your application for vulnerabilities. These tools can identify common security issues and provide recommendations for remediation.

Popular Security Testing Tools:

- **OWASP ZAP**: An open-source web application security scanner.
- **Burp Suite**: A popular tool for web application security testing.

2. Static Code Analysis

Static code analysis tools analyze code without executing it to identify potential vulnerabilities. Integrating static analysis into your CI/CD pipeline can help catch security issues early.

Example: Using SonarQube SonarQube is a popular tool for continuous inspection of code quality, including security vulnerabilities.

3. Dependency Scanning

Regularly scan your dependencies for known vulnerabilities. Tools like **Snyk** or **Dependabot** can help identify outdated packages and known security issues.

Section 6: Monitoring and Incident Response

Once your application is deployed, ongoing monitoring and an effective incident response plan are crucial to maintaining security.

1. Monitoring for Security Incidents

Implement logging and monitoring solutions to detect suspicious activities and security incidents.

Example: Using Application Insights for Monitoring Azure Application Insights can help you monitor the performance and usage of your application, providing insights into potential security issues.

2. Incident Response Plan

Prepare an incident response plan to handle security breaches effectively. This plan should outline steps for identifying, containing, eradicating, and recovering from security incidents.

Key Components of an Incident Response Plan:

- **Preparation**: Develop a plan and ensure all team members are trained.
- **Identification**: Monitor systems for signs of security breaches.
- **Containment**: Limit the impact of a security breach.
- **Eradication**: Remove the cause of the breach.
- **Recovery**: Restore systems to normal operation.
- **Post-Incident Review**: Analyze the incident to prevent future occur-

rences.

Conclusion

In this chapter, we explored the critical topic of security in Clean Architecture applications. We discussed the importance of security, best practices for implementing authentication and authorization, strategies for protecting sensitive data, and common vulnerabilities and their mitigations.

By integrating security into every layer of your Clean Architecture application and following best practices, you can build robust applications that protect user data and maintain trust. In the next chapter, we will delve into advanced topics such as event-driven architecture and integrating messaging systems into your Clean Architecture application.

Chapter 11: Event-Driven Architecture and Messaging in Clean Architecture

Introduction

Event-driven architecture (EDA) is a software architectural paradigm that promotes the production, detection, consumption, and reaction to events. In a Clean Architecture context, EDA enhances the decoupling of components and allows for more scalable and maintainable applications.

In this chapter, you will learn:
- The principles and benefits of event-driven architecture.
- How to implement event-driven systems in .NET applications.
- The role of messaging systems in facilitating communication between components.
- Best practices for using events and messaging in Clean Architecture.

By the end of this chapter, you will have a solid understanding of how to integrate event-driven architecture and messaging into your Clean Architecture applications.

CHAPTER 11: EVENT-DRIVEN ARCHITECTURE AND MESSAGING IN CLEAN...

Section 1: Understanding Event-Driven Architecture

Event-driven architecture is characterized by the production and consumption of events as the primary means of communication between components.

1. What is an Event?

An event is a significant change in state or an occurrence within a system that can trigger reactions from other components. Events can be generated by user actions, system processes, or external systems.

2. Key Principles of Event-Driven Architecture

- **Decoupling**: Components in an event-driven system are loosely coupled, meaning they do not need to know about each other. They communicate via events rather than direct method calls.
- **Asynchronicity**: Events are typically processed asynchronously, allowing systems to react to events without blocking execution. This improves responsiveness and scalability.
- **Scalability**: EDA enables better scaling strategies as events can be processed in parallel across multiple consumers.

3. Benefits of Event-Driven Architecture

- **Improved Responsiveness**: Applications can react quickly to changes and events, improving user experience.
- **Scalability**: EDA allows for easy scaling of components as needed, helping handle increased load efficiently.
- **Flexibility**: New event consumers can be added or modified without impacting existing components, allowing for easier evolution of the system.

Section 2: Implementing Event-Driven Architecture in .NET

Implementing event-driven architecture in .NET can be achieved using various libraries and frameworks that facilitate event handling and messaging.

1. Using .NET Events and Delegates

In .NET, you can use events and delegates for simple event-driven communication within applications.

Example: Implementing a Simple Event in .NET

```csharp
Copy code
public class OrderService
{
    public event EventHandler<OrderCreatedEventArgs> OrderCreated;

    public void CreateOrder(Order order)
    {
        // Logic to create order
        OnOrderCreated(new OrderCreatedEventArgs(order));
    }

    protected virtual void OnOrderCreated(OrderCreatedEventArgs e)
    {
        OrderCreated?.Invoke(this, e);
    }
}

public class OrderCreatedEventArgs : EventArgs
{
    public Order Order { get; }

    public OrderCreatedEventArgs(Order order)
    {
        Order = order;
    }
}
```

2. Using Messaging Systems

CHAPTER 11: EVENT-DRIVEN ARCHITECTURE AND MESSAGING IN CLEAN...

For larger applications, using a messaging system can facilitate better decoupling and more robust event handling. Popular messaging systems include RabbitMQ, Apache Kafka, and Azure Service Bus.

Example: Implementing RabbitMQ in .NET

1. **Install RabbitMQ Client Library**:

```bash
Copy code
dotnet add package RabbitMQ.Client
```

1. **Publish Messages**:

```csharp
Copy code
public class RabbitMqPublisher
{
    private readonly IConnection _connection;
    private readonly IModel _channel;

    public RabbitMqPublisher(string hostname)
    {
        var factory = new ConnectionFactory() { HostName = hostname };
        _connection = factory.CreateConnection();
        _channel = _connection.CreateModel();
        _channel.QueueDeclare(queue: "orders", durable: false,
        exclusive: false, autoDelete: false, arguments: null);
    }

    public void Publish(Order order)
    {
        var json = JsonSerializer.Serialize(order);
```

```csharp
        var body = Encoding.UTF8.GetBytes(json);

        _channel.BasicPublish(exchange: "", routingKey: "orders",
        basicProperties: null, body: body);
    }
}
```

1. **Consume Messages**:

```
csharp
Copy code
public class RabbitMqConsumer
{
    private readonly IConnection _connection;
    private readonly IModel _channel;

    public RabbitMqConsumer(string hostname)
    {
        var factory = new ConnectionFactory() { HostName =
        hostname };
        _connection = factory.CreateConnection();
        _channel = _connection.CreateModel();
        _channel.QueueDeclare(queue: "orders", durable: false,
        exclusive: false, autoDelete: false, arguments: null);
    }

    public void Consume()
    {
        var consumer = new EventingBasicConsumer(_channel);
        consumer.Received += (model, ea) =>
        {
            var body = ea.Body.ToArray();
            var message = Encoding.UTF8.GetString(body);
            var order = JsonSerializer.Deserialize<Order>(message);
            // Process order...
        };
        _channel.BasicConsume(queue: "orders", autoAck: true,
```

```
        consumer: consumer);
    }
}
```

Section 3: Event Sourcing and CQRS

Event sourcing and Command Query Responsibility Segregation (CQRS) are architectural patterns that complement event-driven architecture.

1. What is Event Sourcing?

Event sourcing involves persisting the state of an application as a sequence of events rather than as the current state. This approach provides a complete history of changes and allows for easier auditing and debugging.

Benefits of Event Sourcing:

- **Audit Trail**: Every change in the system is recorded as an event, providing a clear audit trail.
- **Flexibility**: Historical events can be replayed to reconstruct the state of the application at any point in time.
- **Scalability**: Event stores can be optimized for append-only operations, improving performance.

2. Implementing Event Sourcing in .NET

Event sourcing can be implemented in .NET by defining aggregate roots that manage their state through events.

Example: Implementing an Aggregate Root with Event Sourcing

```csharp
Copy code
public class Order
{
    private readonly List<OrderEvent> _events = new
    List<OrderEvent>();
```

```
    public IEnumerable<OrderEvent> Events => _events;

    public void CreateOrder(string customerId, decimal amount)
    {
        var orderCreatedEvent = new OrderCreatedEvent(customerId,
        amount);
        _events.Add(orderCreatedEvent);
        // Apply business logic...
    }
}
```

3. What is CQRS?

CQRS separates the read and write sides of an application, allowing for different models for querying and modifying data. This separation can improve performance and scalability.

Benefits of CQRS:

- **Optimized Read and Write Models**: Tailor each model to its purpose, improving performance.
- **Scalability**: Scale read and write operations independently.
- **Simplified Maintenance**: Reduces complexity in each model by focusing on specific concerns.

4. Implementing CQRS in .NET

Implementing CQRS involves defining separate commands and queries.

Example: Creating Command and Query Handlers

```csharp
Copy code
public class CreateOrderCommand
{
    public string CustomerId { get; }
    public decimal Amount { get; }
```

```csharp
    public CreateOrderCommand(string customerId, decimal amount)
    {
        CustomerId = customerId;
        Amount = amount;
    }
}

public class CreateOrderCommandHandler :
IRequestHandler<CreateOrderCommand>
{
    public async Task<Unit> Handle(CreateOrderCommand request,
    CancellationToken cancellationToken)
    {
        // Handle order creation logic
        return Unit.Value;
    }
}
```

Section 4: Event-Driven Architecture with ASP.NET Core

Integrating event-driven architecture into your ASP.NET Core application involves using middleware and service registrations effectively.

1. Setting Up Middleware for Events

ASP.NET Core allows you to define middleware that can handle events in your application pipeline.

Example: Creating Middleware for Event Handling

```csharp
Copy code
public class EventMiddleware
{
    private readonly RequestDelegate _next;

    public EventMiddleware(RequestDelegate next)
    {
        _next = next;
```

```
    }

    public async Task InvokeAsync(HttpContext context)
    {
        // Logic to handle incoming events
        await _next(context);
    }
}
```

2. Registering Services for Event Handling

You can register event handling services in your Startup.cs.

```csharp
Copy code
public void ConfigureServices(IServiceCollection services)
{
    services.AddSingleton<RabbitMqPublisher>();
    services.AddSingleton<RabbitMqConsumer>();
}
```

Section 5: Challenges of Event-Driven Architecture

While event-driven architecture offers many benefits, it also comes with its own set of challenges that developers must address.

1. Complexity

Managing events can lead to increased complexity in the application. Ensuring that all components correctly produce, consume, and handle events requires careful design.

2. Event Ordering and Consistency

Ensuring that events are processed in the correct order and maintaining data consistency across different systems can be challenging, especially in distributed environments.

3. Debugging and Monitoring

Tracking the flow of events through the system for debugging purposes can be difficult. Implementing effective logging and monitoring strategies is essential.

Section 6: Monitoring and Logging in Event-Driven Systems

Effective monitoring and logging are crucial for understanding the behavior of an event-driven architecture.

1. Implementing Centralized Logging

Using a centralized logging solution allows you to aggregate logs from various components of your application. Tools like **Serilog**, **ELK Stack**, or **Azure Application Insights** can be used.

Example: Configuring Serilog for Centralized Logging

```csharp
Copy code
Log.Logger = new LoggerConfiguration()
    .Enrich.WithProperty("Application", "MyApp")
    .WriteTo.Console()
    .WriteTo.File("logs/app.log", rollingInterval:
    RollingInterval.Day)
    .CreateLogger();

app.UseSerilogRequestLogging();
```

2. Monitoring Event Processing

Implement monitoring to track the performance of event consumers and detect failures. Use APM tools to gain insights into how well your event-driven system is performing.

Conclusion

In this chapter, we explored event-driven architecture and messaging in the context of Clean Architecture. We discussed the principles and benefits of EDA, how to implement it using messaging systems like RabbitMQ, and the role of event sourcing and CQRS.

By leveraging event-driven architecture, you can create scalable, responsive applications that effectively handle complex business scenarios. In the next chapter, we will focus on integrating external services and third-party APIs into your Clean Architecture application, ensuring that your application can extend its functionality and interact with other systems seamlessly.

Chapter 12: Integrating External Services and Third-Party APIs in Clean Architecture

Introduction

In today's interconnected world, applications often need to communicate with external services and third-party APIs to enhance their functionality. Whether it's fetching data, sending notifications, or integrating with payment processors, effectively managing these interactions is crucial for a robust application architecture.

In this chapter, you will learn:
- The principles of integrating external services in Clean Architecture.
- How to design your application for external service interactions.
- Best practices for consuming and managing APIs.
- Techniques for handling failures and timeouts in external calls.
- Strategies for testing external integrations.

By the end of this chapter, you will have a solid understanding of how to integrate external services and third-party APIs into your Clean Architecture applications, ensuring maintainability and scalability.

Section 1: Principles of Integrating External Services

Integrating external services involves several key principles to ensure that your application remains maintainable, scalable, and secure.

1. Decoupling

Ensure that your application components are decoupled from the external services. This can be achieved by defining interfaces that represent the external services, allowing you to swap out implementations without affecting the rest of the application.

2. Abstraction

Create abstractions for external service interactions. This could involve using service classes or repositories that encapsulate the logic for interacting with external APIs. This keeps the business logic clean and free from direct dependencies on external services.

3. Resilience

Design your application to be resilient to external service failures. Implement strategies such as retries, fallbacks, and circuit breakers to handle potential issues gracefully.

4. Security

When interacting with external services, it is crucial to protect sensitive data, such as API keys and user credentials. Use secure methods for storing and transmitting this data.

Section 2: Designing Your Application for External Service Integration

When integrating external services, it's essential to design your application architecture to accommodate these interactions smoothly.

1. Define Interfaces for External Services

Create interfaces that define the methods for interacting with external services. This helps to decouple the implementation from the application logic.

Example: Defining an IWeatherService Interface

```csharp
Copy code
public interface IWeatherService
{
    Task<WeatherForecast> GetWeatherAsync(string location);
}
```

2. Implementing the Service

Create a concrete implementation of the interface that handles the actual interaction with the external API.

Example: Implementing the WeatherService

```csharp
Copy code
public class WeatherService : IWeatherService
{
    private readonly HttpClient _httpClient;

    public WeatherService(HttpClient httpClient)
    {
        _httpClient = httpClient;
    }

    public async Task<WeatherForecast> GetWeatherAsync(string location)
    {
        var response = await _httpClient.GetAsync($"weather?location={location}");
        response.EnsureSuccessStatusCode();

        var weatherData = await response.Content.ReadFromJsonAsync<WeatherForecast>();
        return weatherData;
    }
}
```

3. Configuring Dependency Injection

Register the external service implementation in your DI container, allowing it to be injected into other components.

```csharp
Copy code
public void ConfigureServices(IServiceCollection services)
{
    services.AddHttpClient<IWeatherService, WeatherService>(client =>
    {
        client.BaseAddress = new Uri("https://api.weather.com/");
        client.DefaultRequestHeaders.Add("Accept",
        "application/json");
    });
}
```

Section 3: Consuming Third-Party APIs

When consuming third-party APIs, it's essential to handle data retrieval and management effectively.

1. Making API Calls

Use the HttpClient class to make asynchronous API calls to external services.

Example: Using HttpClient to Call an API

```csharp
Copy code
public async Task<WeatherForecast> GetWeatherAsync(string location)
{
    var response = await
    _httpClient.GetAsync($"weather?location={location}");

    if (response.IsSuccessStatusCode)
    {
        return await
        response.Content.ReadFromJsonAsync<WeatherForecast>();
```

```
    }

    throw new HttpRequestException($"Error fetching weather data:
    {response.StatusCode}");
}
```

2. Handling API Responses

Handle various response scenarios to ensure your application behaves correctly when interacting with external services.

- **Successful Responses**: Process and return the data.
- **Error Responses**: Log the error and throw appropriate exceptions.
- **Timeouts**: Implement retries or fallback strategies for timeouts.

Example: Handling API Response Errors

```csharp
Copy code
if (response.StatusCode == HttpStatusCode.NotFound)
{
    throw new NotFoundException("Weather data not found for the
    specified location.");
}
else if (response.StatusCode == HttpStatusCode.InternalServerError)
{
    // Log error and retry
}
```

Section 4: Resilience and Fault Tolerance

When integrating external services, your application must be resilient to failures and capable of handling various fault scenarios.

1. Implementing Retry Logic

Retry logic allows your application to attempt a failed operation again, which can be beneficial for transient errors.

Example: Using Polly for Retry Logic Polly is a popular resilience and transient-fault-handling library for .NET.

1. **Install the Polly Package**:

```bash
Copy code
dotnet add package Polly
```

1. **Implementing Retry Logic with Polly**

```csharp
Copy code
public async Task<WeatherForecast> GetWeatherWithRetryAsync(string location)
{
    var policy = Policy
        .Handle<HttpRequestException>()
        .WaitAndRetryAsync(3, retryAttempt =>
        TimeSpan.FromSeconds(Math.Pow(2, retryAttempt)));

    return await policy.ExecuteAsync(() =>
    GetWeatherAsync(location));
}
```

2. Circuit Breaker Pattern

The circuit breaker pattern prevents your application from repeatedly attempting to execute an operation that is likely to fail, allowing it to recover.

Example: Implementing a Circuit Breaker with Polly

```csharp
Copy code
var circuitBreakerPolicy = Policy
    .Handle<HttpRequestException>()
    .CircuitBreakerAsync(2, TimeSpan.FromMinutes(1)); // Break
        after 2 failures

return await circuitBreakerPolicy.ExecuteAsync(() =>
GetWeatherAsync(location));
```

Section 5: Testing External Service Integrations

Testing external integrations can be challenging, but it is essential for ensuring that your application behaves correctly.

1. Mocking External Services

Use mocking frameworks like Moq or NSubstitute to create mock implementations of external services for unit testing.

Example: Mocking IWeatherService with Moq

```csharp
Copy code
var mockWeatherService = new Mock<IWeatherService>();
mockWeatherService.Setup(service =>
service.GetWeatherAsync(It.IsAny<string>()))
    .ReturnsAsync(new WeatherForecast { Temperature = 75,
    Condition = "Sunny" });
```

2. Integration Testing External APIs

For integration testing, ensure that your application can successfully interact with the external API in a controlled environment.

Example: Using a Test Environment Use a test environment or a dedicated API testing tool (like Postman or Swagger) to validate that your application integrates correctly with the external service.

3. End-to-End Testing

Conduct end-to-end testing to verify that the entire application works as expected when integrated with external services.

Section 6: Security Considerations for External Integrations

Integrating external services poses security risks that must be addressed to protect sensitive data and application integrity.

1. Secure API Keys and Credentials

Store API keys and credentials securely, using environment variables or secret management tools.

Example: Using Azure Key Vault

```csharp
Copy code
builder.Services.AddAzureKeyVault(Configuration["KeyVault:Url"]);
```

2. Rate Limiting

Implement rate limiting to control the number of requests sent to external services, preventing abuse and ensuring compliance with service limitations.

Example: Using ASP.NET Core Middleware for Rate Limiting

```csharp
Copy code
app.Use(async (context, next) =>
{
    // Implement rate limiting logic here
    await next.Invoke();
});
```

3. Data Protection

Ensure that sensitive data sent to and from external services is encrypted and transmitted securely. Use HTTPS for all API calls.

Section 7: Monitoring and Logging External Integrations

Monitoring and logging are crucial for understanding the behavior of your application when interacting with external services.

1. Centralized Logging for API Calls

Log all API calls, including request and response data, to help diagnose issues and track performance.

Example: Using Serilog for Logging

```csharp
Copy code
public class WeatherService
{
    private readonly ILogger<WeatherService> _logger;

    public WeatherService(ILogger<WeatherService> logger)
    {
        _logger = logger;
    }

    public async Task<WeatherForecast> GetWeatherAsync(string location)
    {
        try
        {
            var response = await
            _httpClient.GetAsync($"weather?location={location}");
            response.EnsureSuccessStatusCode();
            var weatherData = await
            response.Content.ReadFromJsonAsync<WeatherForecast>();
            return weatherData;
        }
        catch (Exception ex)
        {
            _logger.LogError($"Error fetching weather data: {ex.Message}");
            throw;
        }
```

}
}

2. Performance Monitoring

Use APM tools to monitor the performance of external API calls and identify bottlenecks or failures.

Conclusion

In this chapter, we explored the integration of external services and third-party APIs in Clean Architecture applications. We discussed the principles of effective integration, best practices for consuming APIs, and strategies for ensuring resilience and fault tolerance. Additionally, we covered the importance of testing, security considerations, and monitoring.

By effectively integrating external services, you can enhance the functionality of your Clean Architecture applications while ensuring maintainability and security. In the next chapter, we will focus on advanced topics such as deploying and maintaining microservices architectures in a Clean Architecture context.

Chapter 13: Deploying and Maintaining Microservices Architectures in Clean Architecture

Introduction

Microservices architecture has gained significant popularity as a way to build scalable and maintainable applications. By breaking down applications into smaller, independent services that communicate over APIs, organizations can achieve greater agility and resilience. However, deploying and maintaining a microservices architecture requires careful planning and execution, particularly in the context of Clean Architecture.

In this chapter, you will learn about:
- The principles and benefits of microservices architecture.
- How to design microservices using Clean Architecture principles.
- Deployment strategies for microservices.
- Techniques for monitoring and maintaining microservices.
- Best practices for ensuring security and resilience.

By the end of this chapter, you will have a solid understanding of how to deploy and maintain microservices architectures while adhering to Clean Architecture principles.

Section 1: Understanding Microservices Architecture

Microservices architecture is an approach to developing software applications as a suite of independently deployable, small, modular services. Each service runs a unique process and communicates through well-defined APIs.

1. **Key Principles of Microservices Architecture**

- **Single Responsibility**: Each microservice should focus on a specific business capability, promoting separation of concerns.
- **Independently Deployable**: Services can be deployed independently, enabling faster release cycles and reduced downtime.
- **Decentralized Data Management**: Each microservice can have its own database, allowing for data storage that fits its specific needs.
- **Inter-Service Communication**: Microservices communicate through lightweight protocols such as HTTP or messaging queues.

2. **Benefits of Microservices Architecture**

- **Scalability**: Individual services can be scaled independently based on demand, optimizing resource utilization.
- **Agility**: Teams can develop, test, and deploy services independently, speeding up the development process.
- **Resilience**: Failure in one service does not directly impact the entire application, leading to improved fault tolerance.
- **Technology Diversity**: Teams can choose the best technology stack for each service, fostering innovation and flexibility.

Section 2: Designing Microservices with Clean Architecture Principles

Designing microservices in a Clean Architecture context involves applying its principles to ensure maintainability, scalability, and separation of concerns.

1. Layered Architecture in Microservices

Each microservice can be designed using Clean Architecture's layered approach, including:

- **Presentation Layer**: Handles user interactions and API requests.
- **Application Layer**: Contains business logic and coordinates application flow.
- **Domain Layer**: Defines the core domain model and business rules.
- **Infrastructure Layer**: Manages data access and external service integration.

2. Defining Service Boundaries

When designing microservices, it is essential to define clear boundaries for each service based on business capabilities. This can be achieved through:

- **Domain-Driven Design (DDD)**: Use DDD principles to identify bounded contexts and establish clear service boundaries.
- **Event Storming**: Collaborate with stakeholders to visualize and define how services will interact and the events that trigger them.

3. Example: Designing a Microservice for Order Management

For an e-commerce application, you might define an Order microservice that manages order processing, including:

- **Entities**: Order, OrderItem, Customer.
- **Business Logic**: Adding items, calculating totals, and processing payments.
- **Integration**: Communicating with Inventory and Payment microser-

vices.

Section 3: Deployment Strategies for Microservices

Deploying microservices requires specific strategies to ensure smooth operations and scalability.

1. Containerization

Containerization allows you to package microservices along with their dependencies, ensuring consistent environments across development, testing, and production.

Using Docker for Containerization:

- Create a Dockerfile for each microservice to define its environment and dependencies.

Example: Dockerfile for Order Microservice

```
dockerfile
Copy code
FROM mcr.microsoft.com/dotnet/aspnet:6.0 AS base
WORKDIR /app
EXPOSE 80

FROM mcr.microsoft.com/dotnet/sdk:6.0 AS build
WORKDIR /src
COPY ["OrderService/OrderService.csproj", "OrderService/"]
RUN dotnet restore "OrderService/OrderService.csproj"
COPY . .
WORKDIR "/src/OrderService"
RUN dotnet build "OrderService.csproj" -c Release -o /app/build

FROM build AS publish
RUN dotnet publish "OrderService.csproj"
 -c Release -o /app/publish

FROM base AS final
```

CHAPTER 13: DEPLOYING AND MAINTAINING MICROSERVICES...

```
WORKDIR /app
COPY --from=publish /app/publish .
ENTRYPOINT ["dotnet", "OrderService.dll"]
```

2. Orchestration with Kubernetes

Kubernetes is a powerful platform for orchestrating containerized applications, providing features for scaling, load balancing, and service discovery.

Setting Up Kubernetes:

- Create Kubernetes manifests (YAML files) for deploying your microservices, defining the desired state for your application.

Example: Kubernetes Deployment Manifest

```yaml
Copy code
apiVersion: apps/v1
kind: Deployment
metadata:
  name: orderservice
spec:
  replicas: 3
  selector:
    matchLabels:
      app: orderservice
  template:
    metadata:
      labels:
        app: orderservice
    spec:
      containers:
      - name: orderservice
        image: yourdockerhubusername/orderservice:latest
        ports:
        - containerPort: 80
---
apiVersion: v1
```

```
kind: Service
metadata:
  name: orderservice
spec:
  type: ClusterIP
  ports:
  - port: 80
    targetPort: 80
  selector:
    app: orderservice
```

3. Service Discovery

Service discovery is essential in microservices architectures to allow services to find and communicate with each other dynamically.

Using Kubernetes for Service Discovery: Kubernetes provides built-in service discovery through its DNS system, allowing services to communicate using their names.

Section 4: Monitoring and Logging Microservices

Effective monitoring and logging are crucial for managing microservices in production.

1. Centralized Logging

Centralized logging tools aggregate logs from all microservices, making it easier to analyze and troubleshoot issues.

Popular Centralized Logging Solutions:

- **ELK Stack (Elasticsearch, Logstash, Kibana)**: A powerful set of tools for collecting, searching, and visualizing logs.
- **Fluentd**: An open-source data collector that helps unify data collection and consumption.

Example: Configuring Serilog with Elasticsearch

```csharp
Copy code
public void ConfigureServices(IServiceCollection services)
{
    Log.Logger = new LoggerConfiguration()
        .Enrich.FromLogContext()
        .WriteTo.Console()
        .WriteTo.Elasticsearch
(new ElasticsearchSinkOptions
(new Uri("http://localhost:9200"))
        {
            AutoRegisterTemplate = true,
        })
        .CreateLogger();

    services.AddLogging(loggingBuilder =>
    loggingBuilder.AddSerilog(dispose: true));
}
```

2. Application Performance Monitoring (APM)

Implement APM tools to monitor the performance of your microservices. These tools can help identify bottlenecks and track response times.

Popular APM Tools:

- **New Relic**: Provides detailed performance metrics for applications.
- **Application Insights**: Offers monitoring capabilities for applications hosted in Azure.

Section 5: Handling Security in Microservices

Security is a critical consideration in microservices architecture, especially with multiple services interacting over the network.

1. Secure API Communication

Ensure that all communication between microservices is secure. Use HTTPS for all API calls and consider implementing mutual TLS for service-to-service communication.

C 10 CLEAN ARCHITECTURE WITH .NET 6

Example: Enforcing HTTPS in ASP.NET Core

```csharp
Copy code
app.UseHttpsRedirection();
```

2. API Gateway for Security Management

An API gateway can act as a single entry point for your microservices, providing a central location for implementing security measures such as authentication, rate limiting, and logging.

Example: Using Ocelot as an API Gateway

```yaml
Copy code
ReRoutes:
- DownstreamPathTemplate: "/api/orders/{everything}"
  DownstreamScheme: "http"
  DownstreamHostAndPorts:
    - Host: "orderservice"
      Port: 80
  UpstreamPathTemplate: "/orders/{everything}"
  UpstreamHttpMethod: [ "Get", "Post" ]
```

3. Implementing Authentication and Authorization

Implement robust authentication and authorization mechanisms across your microservices. This can involve using OAuth 2.0 or JWT tokens for securing APIs.

Example: Securing Microservices with JWT

```csharp
Copy code
services.AddAuthentication(JwtBearerDefaults.AuthenticationScheme)
    .AddJwtBearer(options =>
    {
        options.TokenValidationParameters = new
```

CHAPTER 13: DEPLOYING AND MAINTAINING MICROSERVICES...

```
        TokenValidationParameters
        {
            ValidateIssuer = true,
            ValidateAudience = true,
            ValidateLifetime = true,
            ValidateIssuerSigningKey = true,
            ValidIssuer = Configuration["Jwt:Issuer"],
            ValidAudience = Configuration["Jwt:Audience"],
            IssuerSigningKey = new
            SymmetricSecurityKey(Encoding.UTF8.
GetBytes(Configuration["Jwt:Key"]))
        };
    });
```

Section 6: Best Practices for Microservices in Clean Architecture

Implementing best practices can help ensure that your microservices architecture remains robust and maintainable.

1. Design for Failure

Assume that failures will occur and design your microservices to handle them gracefully. Use patterns such as circuit breakers and retries to manage transient failures.

2. Versioning APIs

Version your APIs to ensure backward compatibility. This allows you to make changes without breaking existing clients.

Example: API Versioning in ASP.NET Core

```csharp
Copy code
services.AddApiVersioning(options =>
{
    options.AssumeDefaultVersionWhenUnspecified = true;
    options.DefaultApiVersion = new ApiVersion(1, 0);
    options.ReportApiVersions = true;
```

});

3. Keep Microservices Focused

Ensure that each microservice has a single responsibility and does not become a "catch-all" service. This promotes maintainability and scalability.

4. Use Event-Driven Communication Where Appropriate

Leverage event-driven communication between microservices for decoupling and to enhance responsiveness.

Conclusion

In this chapter, we explored the integration of microservices architecture within the context of Clean Architecture. We discussed the principles of microservices, how to design and deploy them effectively, and best practices for monitoring and maintaining these services.

By leveraging microservices, you can build scalable, resilient applications that meet the demands of modern software development. In the next chapter, we will focus on advanced topics such as implementing serverless architecture and exploring its integration with Clean Architecture principles.

Chapter 14: Implementing Serverless Architecture in Clean Architecture

Introduction

Serverless architecture has emerged as a popular approach to building applications, allowing developers to focus on writing code without managing the underlying infrastructure. In a serverless model, cloud providers automatically handle server provisioning, scaling, and maintenance. This chapter explores how to implement serverless architecture in the context of Clean Architecture principles, ensuring that applications remain modular, maintainable, and scalable.

In this chapter, you will learn about:
- The principles of serverless architecture.
- How to design serverless applications using Clean Architecture.
- Implementing serverless functions with Azure Functions or AWS Lambda.
- Best practices for deploying and managing serverless applications.
- Monitoring and troubleshooting serverless solutions.

By the end of this chapter, you will have a solid understanding of how to integrate serverless architecture into your Clean Architecture applications, enabling greater agility and responsiveness.

Section 1: Understanding Serverless Architecture

Serverless architecture is a cloud computing execution model where the cloud provider dynamically manages the allocation of machine resources. Developers can deploy code without worrying about server management.

1. Key Principles of Serverless Architecture

- **Event-Driven**: Serverless applications are often triggered by events, such as HTTP requests, scheduled tasks, or changes in data storage.
- **Pay-as-You-Go**: Billing is based on the actual usage of resources, allowing for cost-effective scaling.
- **Statelessness**: Serverless functions are typically stateless, meaning they do not retain state between executions. Any required state should be stored externally, such as in databases or caches.

2. Benefits of Serverless Architecture

- **Reduced Operational Overhead**: Developers can focus on writing business logic rather than managing servers, leading to faster development cycles.
- **Automatic Scaling**: Serverless applications can automatically scale based on demand, handling sudden spikes in traffic seamlessly.
- **Cost Efficiency**: Pay only for the compute resources consumed during function execution, reducing costs associated with idle resources.

3. Challenges of Serverless Architecture

- **Cold Starts**: When a serverless function is not in use, it may take longer to execute the first time it is invoked due to initialization overhead.
- **Vendor Lock-In**: Relying on a specific cloud provider can lead to challenges if you need to migrate to another platform.
- **Limited Execution Time**: Serverless functions typically have a maximum execution time, which may not be suitable for long-running

CHAPTER 14: IMPLEMENTING SERVERLESS ARCHITECTURE IN CLEAN...

processes.

Section 2: Designing Serverless Applications with Clean Architecture

When implementing serverless architecture, it's essential to design your applications with Clean Architecture principles to maintain modularity and separation of concerns.

1. Defining Service Boundaries

Identify distinct business capabilities that can be implemented as serverless functions. Each function should encapsulate a single responsibility, promoting separation of concerns.

Example: Order Processing Microservice

- **Functions**:
  - CreateOrder: Handles new order creation.
  - ProcessPayment: Manages payment processing.
  - SendOrderConfirmation: Sends confirmation emails after order processing.

2. Layered Architecture in Serverless Functions

While serverless functions are typically single entry points, you can still apply Clean Architecture principles within each function.

- **Presentation Layer**: Handles incoming requests and prepares responses.
- **Application Layer**: Contains business logic and orchestrates the workflow.
- **Domain Layer**: Defines the core domain model and business rules.
- **Infrastructure Layer**: Manages data access and external service interactions.

Example: Structure of a Serverless Function

```plaintext
Copy code
OrderProcessingFunction
│
├── Presentation
│   └── HttpTrigger.cs
├── Application
│   ├── Commands
│   │   └── CreateOrderCommand.cs
│   └── Services
│       └── OrderService.cs
├── Domain
│   └── Entities
│       └── Order.cs
└── Infrastructure
    ├── Repositories
    │   └── OrderRepository.cs
    └── ExternalServices
        └── PaymentService.cs
```

Section 3: Implementing Serverless Functions

Implementing serverless functions involves creating the actual function code, setting up triggers, and managing dependencies.

1. Setting Up Azure Functions

Azure Functions is a serverless compute service that allows you to run code on demand without explicitly managing infrastructure.

Creating an Azure Function:

1. **Install Azure Functions Core Tools**:

CHAPTER 14: IMPLEMENTING SERVERLESS ARCHITECTURE IN CLEAN...

```bash
Copy code
npm install -g azure-functions-core-tools@3 --unsafe-perm true
```

1. **Create a New Function App**:

```bash
Copy code
func init MyFunctionApp --dotnet
```

1. **Add a New Function**:

```bash
Copy code
cd MyFunctionApp
func new --name CreateOrderFunction --template "HTTP trigger"
```

2. Writing the Function Code

Inside the CreateOrderFunction.cs, you can implement the logic for handling order creation.

Example: Implementing an HTTP Trigger Function

```csharp
Copy code
[FunctionName("CreateOrderFunction")]
public async Task<IActionResult> Run(
    [HttpTrigger(AuthorizationLevel.Function, "post", Route = "orders")] HttpRequest req,
    ILogger log)
```

```csharp
{
    log.LogInformation("Processing a new order request.");

    string requestBody = await new
    StreamReader(req.Body).ReadToEndAsync();
    var order = JsonConvert.DeserializeObject<Order>(requestBody);

    // Call application service to process the order
    await _orderService.CreateOrderAsync(order);

    return new CreatedResult($"/orders/{order.Id}", order);
}
```

3. Setting Up Dependency Injection

Azure Functions supports dependency injection, allowing you to manage dependencies and services easily.

Example: Configuring Dependency Injection In your Startup.cs, configure services for your Azure Function app.

```
csharp
Copy code
[assembly: FunctionsStartup(typeof(MyFunctionApp.Startup))]
namespace MyFunctionApp
{
    public class Startup : FunctionsStartup
    {
        public override void Configure(IFunctionsHostBuilder builder)
        {
            builder.Services.AddSingleton<IOrderService, OrderService>();
            builder.Services.AddSingleton<IOrderRepository, OrderRepository>();
        }
    }
}
```

CHAPTER 14: IMPLEMENTING SERVERLESS ARCHITECTURE IN CLEAN...

Section 4: Deploying Serverless Functions

Deploying serverless functions to the cloud involves configuring deployment settings and using tools to facilitate the process.

1. Deploying to Azure

Azure Functions can be deployed using various methods, including the Azure CLI, Visual Studio, or GitHub Actions.

Deploying Using Azure CLI:

1. **Login to Azure**:

```bash
Copy code
az login
```

1. **Create a Resource Group**:

```bash
Copy code
az group create --name MyResourceGroup --location eastus
```

1. **Create a Function App**:

```bash
Copy code
az functionapp create --resource-group MyResourceGroup
--consumption-plan-location eastus --runtime dotnet
--functions-version 3 --name MyFunctionApp
```

1. **Deploy the Function**:

```bash
Copy code
func azure functionapp publish MyFunctionApp
```

2. Continuous Deployment for Serverless Functions

Implementing continuous deployment (CD) pipelines can automate the deployment of your serverless functions.

Using GitHub Actions for CI/CD: Create a GitHub Actions workflow file (.github/workflows/ci-cd.yml) for deploying your Azure Functions automatically upon changes.

```yaml
Copy code
name: CI/CD for Azure Functions

on:
  push:
    branches:
      - main

jobs:
  build:
    runs-on: ubuntu-latest
    steps:
      - name: Checkout Code
        uses: actions/checkout@v2

      - name: Setup .NET Core
        uses: actions/setup-dotnet@v1
        with:
          dotnet-version: '6.0.x'

      - name: Restore Dependencies
        run: dotnet restore
```

CHAPTER 14: IMPLEMENTING SERVERLESS ARCHITECTURE IN CLEAN...

```
- name: Publish to Azure
  run: dotnet publish --configuration Release --output
  ./publish
  env:
    AZURE_FUNCTIONAPP_NAME: ${{
    secrets.AZURE_FUNCTIONAPP_NAME }}
    AZURE_FUNCTIONAPP_PUBLISH_PROFILE: ${{
    secrets.AZURE_FUNCTIONAPP_PUBLISH_PROFILE }}
```

Section 5: Monitoring and Managing Serverless Applications

Monitoring and managing serverless applications is essential for maintaining performance and ensuring reliability.

1. Application Insights for Monitoring

Azure Application Insights provides powerful monitoring capabilities for serverless applications, offering insights into performance, usage, and exceptions.

Configuring Application Insights:

- Add Application Insights to your function app in the Azure portal or via code.

Example: Integrating Application Insights in Azure Functions

```csharp
csharp
Copy code
public class Startup : FunctionsStartup
{
    public override void Configure(IFunctionsHostBuilder builder)
    {
        builder.Services.AddApplicationInsightsTelemetry();
    }
}
```

2. Log Management

Centralized logging helps track the behavior of your serverless functions. Use a logging library like Serilog to send logs to a central location.

Example: Configuring Serilog with Azure Application Insights

```csharp
Copy code
Log.Logger = new LoggerConfiguration()
    .WriteTo.Console()
    .WriteTo.ApplicationInsights(new TelemetryConfiguration {
    InstrumentationKey = "your-instrumentation-key" },
    TelemetryConverter.Events)
    .CreateLogger();
```

3. Performance Monitoring

Monitor the performance of your serverless functions using metrics such as execution duration, success rates, and request counts. This data can help identify bottlenecks and optimize performance.

Section 6: Best Practices for Serverless Architecture in Clean Architecture

Implementing best practices can ensure that your serverless applications remain scalable, maintainable, and resilient.

1. Design for Scalability

Design your serverless functions to handle varying workloads. Use asynchronous programming and batch processing to improve performance.

2. Optimize Cold Starts

To minimize cold start latency, keep your functions warm by using scheduled triggers or configuring a minimum instance count where supported.

3. Implement Circuit Breaker Patterns

Use circuit breaker patterns to gracefully handle failures in dependent services, preventing cascading failures across your serverless application.

4. Maintain Clean Code

Keep your code clean and modular by applying Clean Architecture prin-

CHAPTER 14: IMPLEMENTING SERVERLESS ARCHITECTURE IN CLEAN...

ciples within your serverless functions. This includes using interfaces, abstractions, and proper separation of concerns.

5. Monitor and Iterate

Continuously monitor your serverless applications and iterate on your design based on performance metrics and user feedback.

Conclusion

In this chapter, we explored how to implement serverless architecture within the context of Clean Architecture principles. We discussed the benefits of serverless solutions, how to design and deploy serverless functions, and best practices for monitoring and managing these applications.

By leveraging serverless architecture, you can build scalable, maintainable applications that respond quickly to changing demands while minimizing operational overhead. In the next chapter, we will focus on exploring advanced topics such as integrating AI and machine learning into your Clean Architecture applications, enabling you to enhance their functionality further.

Chapter 15: Integrating AI and Machine Learning into Clean Architecture Applications

Introduction

Artificial Intelligence (AI) and Machine Learning (ML) are transforming the way applications are developed and deployed, enabling smarter features and insights from data. Integrating AI and ML into your Clean Architecture applications can enhance functionality, improve user experiences, and drive better decision-making.

In this chapter, you will learn about:
- The fundamentals of AI and machine learning.
- How to integrate AI and ML models into Clean Architecture.
- Best practices for designing and implementing AI solutions.
- Tools and frameworks for developing machine learning applications in .NET.
- Strategies for monitoring and maintaining AI models in production.

By the end of this chapter, you will have a solid understanding of how to incorporate AI and machine learning into your Clean Architecture applications, enabling you to build innovative and intelligent systems.

CHAPTER 15: INTEGRATING AI AND MACHINE LEARNING INTO CLEAN...

Section 1: Understanding AI and Machine Learning

Before diving into implementation, it is essential to understand the concepts and technologies that underpin AI and machine learning.

1. What is Artificial Intelligence?

Artificial Intelligence refers to the simulation of human intelligence processes by machines, particularly computer systems. These processes include learning (acquiring information and rules for using it), reasoning (using rules to reach approximate or definite conclusions), and self-correction.

2. What is Machine Learning?

Machine Learning is a subset of AI that involves training algorithms to learn from and make predictions based on data. Unlike traditional programming, where explicit instructions are given, machine learning models improve their performance as they are exposed to more data.

Key Concepts in Machine Learning:

- **Supervised Learning**: The model is trained on labeled data, learning to predict the output from input features.
- **Unsupervised Learning**: The model works with unlabeled data to find patterns and groupings.
- **Reinforcement Learning**: The model learns by receiving feedback from its actions, optimizing its behavior to maximize rewards.

Section 2: Designing AI and ML Solutions within Clean Architecture

When integrating AI and ML into a Clean Architecture application, it's crucial to maintain the principles of separation of concerns and modularity.

1. Layering AI Components

You can treat AI components similarly to other application layers, ensuring they adhere to Clean Architecture principles.

- **Presentation Layer**: Handles user interactions, such as inputs for prediction models.

- **Application Layer**: Coordinates the execution of AI/ML models and integrates them into the application workflow.
- **Domain Layer**: Contains business rules related to the AI functions and may involve domain-specific models.
- **Infrastructure Layer**: Manages data access, model storage, and communication with external AI services.

2. Defining Model Interfaces

Create interfaces that define the expected behavior of your AI models. This allows for flexibility and easier testing.

Example: Defining an IRecommendationService Interface

```csharp
Copy code
public interface IRecommendationService
{
    Task<IEnumerable<Product>> GetRecommendationsAsync(User user);
}
```

3. Implementing Machine Learning Models

You can implement machine learning models in various ways, such as:

- Training models using libraries like ML.NET.
- Integrating pre-trained models using tools like ONNX (Open Neural Network Exchange).

Example: Implementing a Recommendation Service with ML.NET

```csharp
Copy code
public class RecommendationService : IRecommendationService
{
    private readonly MLContext _mlContext;
    private readonly ITransformer _model;
```

```
public RecommendationService()
{
    _mlContext = new MLContext();
    _model = LoadModel("model.zip");
}

public async Task<IEnumerable<Product>>
GetRecommendationsAsync(User user)
{
    var predictionEngine =
    _mlContext.Model.CreatePredictionEngine<User,
    RecommendationPrediction>(_model);
    var prediction = predictionEngine.Predict(user);

    return prediction.RecommendedProducts;
}
}
```

Section 3: Training Machine Learning Models

Training machine learning models is a crucial step in building AI solutions. This section covers the training process and considerations.

1. Data Collection and Preparation

The success of machine learning models heavily relies on the quality of data. Collect and preprocess data to ensure it is clean and relevant.

Data Preprocessing Steps:

- **Data Cleaning**: Remove inconsistencies and missing values.
- **Feature Engineering**: Transform raw data into features that better represent the underlying problem.
- **Normalization/Standardization**: Scale the data to improve the performance of algorithms.

Example: Using ML.NET for Data Preparation

```csharp
Copy code
public class UserData
{
    public float Age { get; set; }
    public float Income { get; set; }
    public string Gender { get; set; }
}

public class ProcessedData
{
    public float[] Features { get; set; }
    public float Label { get; set; }
}

// Load and preprocess data
var dataView = _mlContext.Data.
LoadFromTextFile<UserData>("data.csv",
 separatorChar: ',', hasHeader: true);
var processedData = dataView
    .Select(row => new ProcessedData
    {
Features = new float[] { row.Age, row.Income },
Label = row.Gender ==
"Male" ? 1f : 0f // Binary classification
    });
```

2. Selecting and Training Models

Choose an appropriate algorithm based on your problem type (e.g., regression, classification, clustering). Train your model using the prepared data.

Example: Training a Model with ML.NET

```csharp
Copy code
var pipeline = _mlContext.Transforms.Concatenate("Features",
nameof(UserData.Age), nameof(UserData.Income))
```

```
    .Append(_mlContext.BinaryClassification.
Trainers.SdcaLogisticRegression
(labelColumnName: "Label",
maximumNumberOfIterations: 100));

var model = pipeline.Fit(processedData);
```

3. Evaluating Model Performance

Evaluate your model's performance using metrics relevant to your problem domain (e.g., accuracy, precision, recall).

Example: Evaluating a Binary Classification Model

```csharp
Copy code
var predictions = model.Transform(testData);
var metrics = _mlContext.
BinaryClassification.Evaluate(predictions);

Console.WriteLine($"Accuracy: {metrics.Accuracy:P2}");
Console.WriteLine($"AUC:
{metrics.AreaUnderRocCurve:P2}");
```

Section 4: Deploying Machine Learning Models

Once trained, your models must be deployed in a way that makes them accessible to your application.

1. Hosting ML Models

You can host machine learning models using various approaches:

- **In-Memory Hosting**: Load the model into memory and serve predictions directly from the application.
- **Model Serving Platforms**: Use platforms like Azure ML, AWS SageMaker, or TensorFlow Serving for scalable model serving.

Example: Hosting a Model with Azure ML

1. **Register the Model**:

```bash
Copy code
az ml model register --name mymodel
--path ./model.zip --resource-group
myResourceGroup --workspace-name myWorkspace
```

1. **Deploy the Model as a Web Service**:

```bash
Copy code
az ml service create --model mymodel:1
--ic inferenceconfig.json
--config deploymentconfig.json
```

2. Consuming ML Models in Clean Architecture

Integrate your hosted models within the Clean Architecture framework, ensuring that application layers remain decoupled.

Example: Consuming a Model as a REST API

```csharp
Copy code
public class PredictionService : IPredictionService
{
    private readonly HttpClient _httpClient;

    public PredictionService(HttpClient httpClient)
    {
        _httpClient = httpClient;
    }

    public async Task<PredictionResult> GetPredictionAsync(InputData inputData)
```

```
{
    var response = await
_httpClient.PostAsJsonAsync("http:
//myapi.com/predict", inputData);
        response.EnsureSuccessStatusCode();

        return await response.Content.ReadFromJsonAsync
<PredictionResult>();
    }
}
```

Section 5: Monitoring and Maintaining AI Models

Monitoring and maintaining your AI models is crucial to ensure their performance and relevance over time.

1. Performance Monitoring

Monitor model performance using metrics that reflect accuracy, response times, and user feedback. Tools like Azure Application Insights can help with monitoring.

2. Retraining Models

Over time, your models may become less effective as data evolves. Implement a strategy for periodically retraining your models with fresh data to maintain accuracy.

Example: Scheduling Retraining Jobs Use Azure Functions or a similar service to automate the retraining of models based on a schedule or specific events.

3. Versioning Models

Version your models to manage changes over time. This allows you to roll back to previous versions if needed and helps track the evolution of your models.

Example: Using Semantic Versioning for Models

```plaintext
Copy code
model_v1.0.0
model_v1.1.0
model_v2.0.0
```

Section 6: Best Practices for Integrating AI and ML

Implementing best practices will help ensure that your AI and ML solutions are effective, maintainable, and scalable.

1. Start Small

Begin with simple models and gradually introduce complexity. Validate your approach before scaling up.

2. Ensure Data Quality

Invest time in ensuring that your training data is of high quality. Poor-quality data can lead to ineffective models.

3. Foster Collaboration

Encourage collaboration between data scientists, developers, and stakeholders to ensure that AI solutions align with business needs.

4. Keep Models Modular

Design models to be modular and reusable. This promotes cleaner code and easier maintenance.

5. Stay Updated with AI Trends

AI and ML technologies are rapidly evolving. Keep abreast of new tools, libraries, and best practices to enhance your applications.

Conclusion

In this chapter, we explored how to integrate AI and machine learning into Clean Architecture applications. We discussed the principles of AI and ML, how to design and deploy models, and best practices for monitoring and maintaining AI solutions.

CHAPTER 15: INTEGRATING AI AND MACHINE LEARNING INTO CLEAN...

By effectively incorporating AI and machine learning, you can build intelligent applications that provide valuable insights and enhance user experiences. In the next chapter, we will focus on exploring advanced topics such as integrating blockchain technology into your Clean Architecture applications, allowing for enhanced security and trust.

Conclusion

As we conclude this exploration of integrating AI and machine learning into Clean Architecture applications, it is essential to reflect on the journey we've undertaken through this chapter and the broader implications for software development in today's rapidly evolving technological landscape.

Embracing AI and Machine Learning

Artificial intelligence and machine learning are no longer mere buzzwords; they are transformative technologies that have reshaped how applications are built and utilized across various industries. By harnessing the power of AI, developers can create systems that not only process data but also learn from it, adapt to changing circumstances, and make intelligent decisions that enhance user experiences and drive business value.

Integration with Clean Architecture

The principles of Clean Architecture serve as a robust foundation for incorporating AI and ML into applications. By applying the core tenets of separation of concerns, modularity, and maintainability, developers can ensure that their AI solutions are not only effective but also sustainable over time.

1. **Decoupling AI Components**:

   - By defining clear interfaces for AI services, we decouple the implementation details from the application logic. This allows for flexibility in swapping out models or integrating new ones without affecting other parts of the system.

1. **Layered Design**:

- The application's layered architecture enables developers to maintain a clean separation between presentation, application, domain, and infrastructure layers. This separation is crucial when integrating complex AI functionalities, ensuring that each component remains focused on its primary responsibility.

1. **Testing and Reliability**:

- With the integration of AI and ML, the testing strategies discussed in earlier chapters become even more critical. Rigorous testing, including unit tests, integration tests, and performance monitoring, helps ensure that the AI models perform reliably under various conditions.

Practical Implementation

Throughout the chapter, we examined the practical aspects of implementing AI and machine learning within the Clean Architecture framework:

- **Model Training and Deployment**:
- We discussed how to prepare data, train models, and deploy them using tools like ML.NET and Azure ML. This hands-on approach empowers developers to build intelligent applications that leverage data effectively.
- **Continuous Improvement**:
- The necessity of monitoring model performance and implementing feedback loops for retraining reinforces the idea that AI is not a one-time implementation but an ongoing process. As data evolves, so too must the models that interpret and act upon it.

Best Practices for AI Integration

The best practices outlined in this chapter provide a roadmap for successfully integrating AI and ML into applications:

- **Start with Simplicity**:
- Focusing on simple models initially allows for quick iterations and learning, which can be built upon as the application's needs grow.
- **Prioritize Data Quality**:
- The importance of high-quality data cannot be overstated. Ensuring that training data is accurate, relevant, and representative is essential for building effective AI models.
- **Collaborative Development**:
- Encouraging collaboration between data scientists, developers, and business stakeholders fosters a deeper understanding of how AI can be applied to meet specific business challenges and user needs.
- **Stay Informed**:
- The field of AI and machine learning is rapidly evolving, and staying informed about new techniques, tools, and methodologies is crucial for maintaining a competitive edge.

Future Prospects

As we move forward into an era increasingly defined by AI-driven applications, the ability to seamlessly integrate these technologies into robust architectures will be paramount. Organizations that embrace AI not only enhance their applications but also position themselves to leverage data in ways that create significant value.

The potential applications of AI and machine learning are vast—ranging from predictive analytics and personalized user experiences to automated decision-making and intelligent resource management. By integrating these technologies thoughtfully and strategically within Clean Architecture frameworks, developers can create systems that are not only powerful but also adaptable to the ever-changing technological landscape.

CONCLUSION

Final Thoughts

In conclusion, the integration of AI and machine learning into Clean Architecture applications is a journey filled with opportunities for innovation and improvement. By following the principles and practices outlined in this chapter, developers can build intelligent systems that harness the full potential of AI while maintaining the structural integrity and flexibility of Clean Architecture. As you embark on this journey, remember that the ultimate goal is to create applications that not only meet current needs but also anticipate future challenges and opportunities, driving continuous improvement and delivering value to users and organizations alike.

As we proceed to the next chapter, we will delve into advanced topics such as integrating blockchain technology into Clean Architecture applications, further expanding the toolkit available for building modern, intelligent systems. Thank you for your commitment to understanding and applying these concepts, and I look forward to our continued exploration of innovative software development practices.

www.ingramcontent.com/pod-product-compliance
Lightning Source LLC
Chambersburg PA
CBHW071026240526
45469CB00006BD/2103